OWN IT! 4

B1 Preliminary (for Schools) test content in Own It! Level 4 has been checked by Cambridge Assessment English for accuracy and level.

STUDENT'S BOOK
WITH DIGITAL PACK

Samantha Lewis and Daniel Vincent
with Andrew Reid

CAMBRIDGE
UNIVERSITY PRESS

CONTENTS

	Vocabulary	Language in action	Reading
Starter Unit Welcome! p4	Travel p4 Music and theatre p4 Ways of communicating p7	Present and past simple and continuous p6 Present perfect and past simple p8	An interview in a school magazine p5
Unit 1 Trendsetters p10	Describing clothes and shoes p11 Verbs related to clothes and shoes p14	Present perfect simple and present perfect continuous p13 Modifiers p15	A blog post: Fashion & technology – Connected clothes p12 A travel guide: Traditional Scottish dress p18 What we wear and why p18
Unit review p20, **Finished?** p118			
Unit 2 Changes p22	Phrasal verbs: changes p23 Parts of objects p26	*used to*, *would* and past simple p25 Past perfect with *never*, *already*, *by (then)*, *by the time* p27	A brochure: ACE Exchanges – discover a new world and a new you! p24 History: Starting again p137
Unit review p32, **Finished?** p119			
Unit 3 Food for thought p34	Cooking verbs p35 Quantities p38	Future tenses p37 Future continuous and future perfect p39	An online forum: class 4C study room p36 An article: A taste of Australia p42 Food in Japan p42
Unit review p44, **Finished?** p120			
Unit 4 Sense and sensitivity p46	The five senses p47 Describing texture, sound, taste, etc. p50	Deduction and possibility p49 Obligation, prohibition, necessity and advice p51	A magazine article: No pain, no fear – No way! p48 Science: Echolocation p138
Unit review p56, **Finished?** p121			
Unit 5 Wonderful world p58	Processes p59 Extreme adjectives p62	The passive p61 Question tags and questions with prepositions p63	A webzine article: Smart cities of the future p60 A travel blog: Scott the Explorer p66 Extreme homes p66
Unit review p68, **Finished?** p122			
Unit 6 No limits p70	Verb collocations with *get*, *take* and *have* p71 Inspiration and challenge p74	First and second conditional p73 Third conditional p75	A fact sheet: When taking risks is a good thing p72 Citizenship: Digital Citizenship: case studies p139
Unit review p80, **Finished?** p123			
Unit 7 Keep calm! p82	Feelings p83 Expressions with *heart* and *mind* p86	Gerunds and infinitives p85 Subject and object questions p87	A magazine interview: The power of 'not yet' p84 A report about schools in Denmark p90 Happiness around the world p90
Unit review p92, **Finished?** p124			
Unit 8 Advertising p94	Advertising p95 Internet verbs p98	Defining and non-defining relative clauses p97 Indefinite, reflexive and reciprocal pronouns p99	A report: Online advertising p96 Art and design: How to design an effective print advert p140
Unit review p104, **Finished?** p125			
Unit 9 Have you heard the news? p106	Reporting verbs p107 Adverbs of time and manner p110	Reported statements and commands p109 Reported questions p111	A newspaper story: International twins! p108 A story: Maori storytelling – How Maui slowed the Sun p114 Stories on stage p114
Unit review p116, **Finished?** p126			

Vocabulary Bank p127–136 CLIL p137–140 Pronunciation p141–142 Irregular verbs p143

Listening	Speaking and pronunciation	Writing	Project	Learn to Learn
A talk p7		An informal email p9		Personalising vocabulary p4 Describing words you don't know with other words or a gesture p7
An interview p14	Giving your opinion politely p16 Everyday English p16 The letters *ea* p141	A blog comment p17		Categorising p11 Recording new verbs p14 Using spidergrams p19 Learn to … write different kinds of example sentences p21
A quiz show p26	Explaining how to use something p28 Everyday English p28 *used to* p141	An opinion essay p29	The history project: a retro museum exhibition p30 *How to* schedule p31	Using words in different situations p23 Identifying key words p26 Learn to … help your partner improve their writing p33
A recipe p38	Giving instructions p40 Everyday English p640 The letters *ch* p141	A listicle p41		Wordbuilding: adjectives from verbs p35 Using diagrams p38 Understanding words from context p43 Learn to … set and achieve learning goals p45
An interview p50	Making guesses and giving clues p52 Everyday English p52 Weak form of *to* p141	An encyclopaedia entry p53	The science project: an infographic on animal senses p54 *How to* research p54	Brainstorming p47 Using visual clues when listening p50 Learn to … plan your homework p57
A virtual reality tour p62	Expressing surprise and disbelief p64 Everyday English p64 The letters *mb* and *bt* p142	A competition entry p65		Learning verbs with prepositions p59 Listening for specific information p62 Skimming for gist p66 Learn to … use a presentation plan p69
A podcast p74	Encouraging a friend to do something p76 Everyday English p76 Stress in multi-syllable words p142	A for and against essay p77	The citizenship project: a leaflet p78 *How to* motivate yourself and your peers p78	Using collocations in sentences p71 Listening and choosing the correct option p74 Learn to … take responsibility for your learning p81
A conversation p86	Expressing sympathy and concern p88 Everyday English p88 Initial consonant clusters with *s* p142	An email reply p89		Remembering adjectives p83 Gapped flashcards p86 Synonyms and antonyms p91 Learn to … give your partner useful feedback p93
An interview p98	Recommending an online tool p100 Everyday English p100 The letters *-tion* p142	An online product review p101	The art and design project: an advert storyboard p102 *How to* give feedback p102	Wordbuilding: nouns and verbs p95 Open-ended questions p98 Learn to … work out the meaning of new words p105
A news report p110	Telling an anecdote p112 Everyday English p112 The letters *cia* p142	A news story p113		Telling stories to remember new words p107 Collaborative listening p110 Irregular adjective and noun pairs p115 Learn to … ask for help when you don't understand p117

STARTER

WELCOME!

VOCABULARY

Travel

S.01 **1 Match the words in the box with the photos. Listen, check and repeat.**

accommodation	☐	backpacking	☐
holiday resort	☐	sightseeing	1
tourist attractions	☐	trip	☐

1 
2 
3 
4 
5 
6 

S.02 **2 Complete the comments with the words in Exercise 1. Listen and check.**

Where did you go on holiday this summer?

London. It's a great city for [1] sightseeing because there are so many [2] __________. My favourite was Big Ben.

To a [3] __________ in Greece. The [4] __________ was amazing – a beautiful hotel right next to the beach.

I went [5] __________ in Mexico this summer – just me, my bag, and a paper map. It was the best [6] __________ of my life.

LEARN TO LEARN

Personalising vocabulary

Writing sentences helps you to remember words.

Use it!

3 Write true sentences about your holidays with the words in Exercise 1.

____

____

____

Music and theatre

S.03 **4 Match the nouns in the box with the definitions. Listen, check and repeat.**

audience lines part ~~rehearsal~~ scene show

1 When people practise a play rehearsal
2 live performance in a theatre __________
3 the words actors say __________
4 a character in a play __________
5 the people who watch __________
6 a part of a play __________

Use it!

5 Complete the questions with words in Exercise 4. Discuss the questions.

1 Have you ever been in a show at school? What __________ did you play? How did you learn your __________? Did you have any __________ before the show?
2 How is the __________ at the theatre and cinema different to at a concert?
3 If you were in a film, would you like to appear all the way through the film, or be in one big, important __________?

Explore it!

Guess the correct answer.

What films do these lines come from?

a 'To infinity and beyond!'
b 'Just keep swimming.'

Write other famous lines from English films. Can your partner guess the film?

READING

An interview in a school magazine

S.04 **1** Look at the photo. What do you think the boy is doing? Read the interview and check your answer.

Now that we're back to school, everybody's talking about what they did in the summer. Some of you probably stayed in a holiday resort or went sightseeing with your family, and most of you probably spent time at the pool with friends. But not Joshua Wills. His summer was very different. Let's find out why.

Joshua, you didn't have a normal summer holiday this year, did you? What did you do?

No, I didn't. I took part in a theatre camp for teenagers. Our teachers were real actors from the theatre and TV. They taught us all about acting – you know, how to develop a character, how to project your voice and use your body. It was lots of fun.

Did you put on a show?

We put on a musical about a detective. I played the part of the detective's assistant. We had one rehearsal every day for a week, and then three performances. Lots of my friends and family came.

How did it go?

It was great, but on the first night, in the final scene, I forgot my lines. Everything was going really well and then suddenly I couldn't remember anything! Everyone in the audience was looking at me, thinking, 'What's wrong? He's not speaking. He's not even moving!'

Were you panicking?

I wasn't panicking. I was just frozen! But in the end I remembered the lines and it was all OK.

Do you want to do more theatre?

Definitely! I don't want to stop. In fact, I'm writing a play. It's more difficult than I expected, but I'm really enjoying it. I want to put it on at school.

Are you looking for any actors?

Of course! Why? Do you want to join us?

Maybe! It sounds like fun!

2 Read the interview again and answer the questions.

1 Why was Joshua's summer holiday unusual?

______

2 What did the theatre camp participants learn?

______

3 How often did the group practise their play?

______

4 What problem did Joshua have?

______

5 How did the audience react to the problem?

______

6 Why is Joshua looking for actors now?

______

3 Find words in the interview that mean:

1 speak loudly and clearly (phrase) ______
2 somebody who helps someone do their job (n) ______
3 unable to move (adj) ______
4 100% yes! (adv) ______

Voice it!

4 Discuss the questions.

1 Joshua's teachers were real actors. What is good about this?
2 Have you ever acted or spoken in front of a big group of people? How was it?

Watch video S.1
What did he do every day?
What's he doing now?

LANGUAGE IN ACTION

Present and past simple and continuous

Present simple	Present continuous	Past simple	Past continuous
It **sounds** like fun.	I [1] ___ **writing** a play.	We **had** one rehearsal every day.	Everybody in the audience [2] ___ **looking** at me.
I [3] ___ **want** to stop.	He **isn't speaking**.	You [4] ___ **have** a normal summer holiday this year.	I [5] ___ **panicking**.
[6] ___ you **want** to try?	[7] ___ you **looking** for actors?	What [8] ___ you **do**?	**Were** you **panicking**?

1 **Complete the examples in the table above with the correct form of *be* or *do*. Use the interview on page 5 to help you.**

S.05 **2** **Complete the sentences with the correct form of the verbs in brackets. Listen and check.**

1. Mike _goes_ (go) sightseeing every year.
2. Amalia ___________ (not learn) her lines until the night before the first show.
3. A Where's Harry? B He ___________ (read) in his room.
4. You didn't like the play, did you, Emir? You ___________ (sleep) during it!
5. I'm so happy we ___________ (not stay) in that holiday resort last week when the terrible storm came.
6. Ana's not at the rehearsal because she ___________ (not feel) well right now.

3 **Complete Esma's blog with the correct form of the verbs in the box.**

begin do get up go ~~have~~ not finish
not forget practise start think

Hi, everyone. Yesterday we [1] _had_ our last rehearsal for the musical. I [2] ______ practising until 11 pm, and when I [3] ______ to bed, some of the others [4] ______ still ______ . The first show [5] ______ at 7.30 tonight. I didn't feel nervous when I [6] ______ this morning, but I [7] ______ to feel nervous now – I hope I [8] ______ my lines. But I'm also really excited. I [9] ______ it's going to be a great night. Anyway, [10] ______ you ______ anything this weekend? Why don't you come and see me?

Use it!

4 **Write the questions.**

1. what / you / do / at nine o'clock last night
   What were you doing at nine o'clock last night?
2. what time / you / get up / today
   ____
3. during the summer / you / prefer to go sightseeing or go to the beach
   ____
4. what time / you / usually / get up / when you're on holiday
   ____
5. speak English to anyone / last week
   ____
6. what / you / wear / at the moment
   ____

5 **Ask and answer the questions.**

What were you doing at nine o'clock last night?

I was watching some videos online.

VOCABULARY AND LISTENING

Ways of communicating

S.06 **1** **Match the verbs in the box with the emoticons 1–9. Listen, check and repeat.**

describe	☐	greet	☐	post	☐
shake hands	1	shout	☐	smile	☐
translate	☐	wave	☐	whisper	☐

S.07 **2** **Listen to the dialogues and circle the correct words in Exercise 1.**

1 whisper / shake hands
2 translate / smile
3 post / shout
4 greet / translate
5 wave / describe

3 **Do we express the verbs in Exercise 1 with actions or words? Complete the table.**

Actions	Words
shake hands	*describe*

LEARN TO LEARN

Describing words you don't know with other words or a gesture

When you don't know a word, use words you do know to describe it or use gestures to express what you mean.

4 **Express or explain the words in the box with other words or gestures.**

accommodation cry dance film frozen
sing stand up tourist attraction

It's a place where you can stay. *Accommodation?*

Use it!

5 **Use gestures or tell your partner *I do this when …* . Can they guess the verb?**

A talk

S.08 **6** **Listen to Mateo and tick (✓) the tips that helped him learn English.**

a Describe a word with other words ☐
b Do a language course ☐
c Don't worry about making mistakes ☐
d Listen to music ☐
e Talk as much as possible ☐
f Translate words and make them sound English ☐
g Watch TV ☐

S.08 **7** **Listen again and complete each sentence with one word.**

1 Mateo is studying ____________ at university.
2 He didn't understand the family at first because they ____________ so fast.
3 When he doesn't know a word, he describes it, ____________ it or makes a word in English similar to the Spanish word.
4 Lots of things were different for him, but he liked the ____________ best.

Voice it!

8 **Discuss the questions.**

1 Which of Mateo's tips do you use?
2 Which tips would you like to try?

Watch video S.2
Where did she go last summer?
Which language has she never studied?

LANGUAGE IN ACTION
Present perfect and past simple

Present perfect	Past simple
I've **been** at university now for three months.	I **started** my course in October.
I **haven't stopped** [1] _____ I was there! I've [2] _____ **been** to London.	I **met** lots of people in the first few weeks.
Have you [3] _____ **been** to London?	**Did** you **go** to London last year?

1 **Complete the examples in the table above with *ever*, *since* or *never*.**

Get it right!

We don't use the present simple with *since*.

*We've **been** here **since** Tuesday.*

NOT ~~*We are here since Tuesday.*~~

2 **Look at sentences a–d. Circle the correct options to complete the rules.**

a Last year I **spent** six months in London.

b I **didn't understand** the kids because they **spoke** fast.

c I**'ve watched** every episode of *The Big Bang Theory*.

d I**'ve stayed** in contact with people I **met** in London.

1 Use the *present perfect* / *past simple* for things that happened in a finished time period, e.g. last year.

2 Use the *present perfect* / *past simple* for things that happened in the past in an unfinished time period, or when the exact time of the action is not important.

S.09 **3** **Circle the correct words. Listen and check.**

BEN [1]*Have you ever been* / *Did you ever go* to a music festival?

JESSIE Yeah, [2]*I've been* / *went* to one this summer. It was great.

BEN Where [3]*has it been* / *was it*?

JESSIE Near the town where we [4]*have been* / *went* on holiday. [5]*We've stayed* / *stayed* in the town lots of times but this was our first time at the festival.

BEN What [6]*have you liked* / *did you like* best?

JESSIE The Night Owls [7]*have had* / *had* some amazing dancers and [8]*have sounded* / *sounded* incredible.

BEN [9]*I've never heard* / *didn't hear* of them.

JESSIE Oh, they're great! [10]*I've liked* / *liked* them for ages.

4 **Complete the text with the past simple or present perfect.**

I [1] _have_ never _been_ (be) to Mexico, but last summer I [2] __________ (get) a job in a Mexican restaurant. I [3] __________ (meet) loads of people since I [4] __________ (start) working there and I [5] __________ (make) friends. At first they [6] __________ (speak) to me in Spanish, but I [7] __________ (not understand). Since then I [8] __________ (go) to Spanish classes and I [9] __________ (learn) lots. Our teacher [10] __________ (teach) us how to describe things when we don't know the exact word.

Use it!

5 **Discuss the questions.**

1 How many cities in your country have you visited?

2 How long have you know your best friend?

3 Have you ever been to a festival?

I've been to three cities. I went to the capital last month, but there are some cities I've never been to.

WRITING

An informal email

1 **Look at the photos. What can you see? Read Azra's email and put the photos in the correct order.**

a  ☐

b  ☐

c  ☐

2 **Read the email again. Why did Azra write the email? What did she enjoy about her visit?**

[1]From:	azra.kara@myemail.com
[2]To:	gaby.bates@myemail.com
[3]Subject:	Thank you

[4]Hi Gaby,

[5]How are things? [6]I just wanted to say thank you for a great visit to Manchester. I had an amazing time and your family are so kind!

I loved meeting your friends and visiting the city. There's so much to see! I learned so much about the UK that I didn't know before. I've listened to the playlist you made me lots of times since I got back home and I know all the words to the songs!

I've told my friends all about my trip and they're really looking forward to meeting you next month. I can't wait to take you sightseeing in Istanbul to show you all the tourist attractions and introduce you to my friends and family. We've bought tickets to go and watch a Turkish dance show while you're here – I hope you like it!

[7]Write back soon,

[8]Love Azra

3 **Match the letters a–h with the parts of the email 1–8.**

a Address of the recipient ☐
b Address of the sender 1
c Ending and your name ☐
d First sentence ☐
e Last sentence ☐
f Reason you are writing ☐
g Beginning and name ☐
h Topic of the email ☐

4 **Complete the *Useful language* box with phrases from the email.**

Useful language

Starting and ending an informal email

Start + name: Hello Gaby / [1] __________

First sentence: How are you? / Thanks for your email / [2] __________ ?

The reason you are writing: I'm writing to / [3] __________

Last sentence: See you soon. / Bye for now. / [4] __________

End + name: Take care, Azra / [5] __________

Write your own informal email to a friend.

PLAN

5 **Imagine you are doing an exchange with someone in an English-speaking country. You have visited their country and they are going to visit yours. Make notes about these things.**

where you went ____________________

what you did ____________________

what you liked about your visit ____________________

what you are going to do when they visit you ____________________

WRITE

6 **Write your email. Remember to include language and vocabulary from this unit, phrases from the *Useful language* box, the parts of the email in Exercise 3 and the ideas in Exercise 5.**

CHECK

7 **Do you …**

- start and end the email correctly?
- give the reason why you are writing?
- say what you are going to do when your friend visits?

1 TRENDSETTERS

LEARNING OUTCOMES

I can ...

- understand texts about technology and fashion
- give my opinion politely
- comment on a blog post
- understand how to use the present perfect simple and continuous and modifiers
- talk about and describe clothes and shoes
- categorise adjectives, record new verbs, use spidergrams for associated words.

Start it!

1 Look at the photo. Do you like the clothes that the people are wearing? Why? / Why not?
2 Before you watch, what does fashion mean to you?
3 Name three ways fashion changed in the 1960s. Watch and check.
4 What is your favourite fashion style?

Watch video 1.1

p13

Language in action 1.2

p15

Language in action 1.3

p16

Everyday English 1.4

p18

Globetrotters 1.5

VOCABULARY
Describing clothes and shoes

1.01 **1** Match the adjectives in **bold** with the numbers in the photos. Listen, check and repeat.

baggy trousers	☐	**checked** shirt	☐
denim skirt	☐	**flat** shoes	☐
flowery dress	☐	**high-heeled** boots	☐
long-sleeved dress	☐	**plain cotton** T-shirt	☐
spotted shoes	☐	**striped** T-shirt	☐
tight jeans	1		

1.02 **2** Juan and Rosa are shopping for clothes for a school party. Listen to the conversation. Which things in Exercise 1 do they buy?

____

____

LEARN TO LEARN

Categorising

When we use lots of adjectives to describe one thing, we use this order: shape, colour, pattern, material.

3 Complete the table with the adjectives in Exercise 1.

Shape	Pattern	Material

4 Write three sentences describing the clothes in Exercise 1. Use at least two adjectives in each sentence.

She's wearing a white cotton T-shirt.

1 ______________________________

2 ______________________________

3 ______________________________

5 Read your sentences in Exercise 4. Can your partner guess which photo you are describing?

Use it!

6 Discuss the questions.

1 Which clothes in Exercise 1 do you have?
2 Can you describe the clothes you are wearing?
3 Which shapes, patterns and materials do you usually wear? Which do you never wear?

Explore it!

Guess the correct answer.

Some celebrities wear special 'anti-paparazzi' scarves. What do you think these scarves do?

a make their faces more beautiful
b make the photos go black
c make the celebrities look ugly

Find out about a clothes designer. Write a question for your partner to answer.

Fashion & technology

CONNECTED CLOTHES

Anyone who has been reading my blog for a while knows that I'm a huge fan of technology in fashion. Here are my latest discoveries.

A We've all seen watches that measure how much we move or sleep, but what about a T-shirt? Over the last few years, scientists have been developing clothes which can record information about our heart rate or breathing and which can help us stay healthy. Most people have a denim jacket. But have you ever seen a denim jacket that can play music or send instant messages? Well, scientists have designed one that can. You just have to touch the sleeve and your music starts playing!

B Scientists have also created clothes with sensors that take our body temperature and circulate warm or cool air through the material so that we never feel too hot or too cold. Special clothes for astronauts or emergency service workers have been using this technology for years, but now companies have created similar materials for everyday clothing and shoes. Great! No more hot, sweaty feet!

C Now there are even smart clothes that produce energy while we're wearing them! Scientists in South Korea have created a material that turns movement into electricity. So, you can charge your phone while you're doing exercise or just walking around! That's smart!

D Finally, if you haven't been following my updates on 3-D printing, check out these trendy designs. My favourite is the high-heeled shoes. I love the fact that each design is individual and that one day we'll be able to design and print our own patterned or plain clothes and shoes at home.

READING

A blog post

1 **Look at the pictures. How do they combine technology and fashion?**

1.03 **2** **Read the blog post. Match headings 1–4 with paragraphs A–D.**

1 3-D printed clothes ____
2 Clothes that change temperature ____
3 Connected clothing ____
4 Energy-producing clothes ____

3 **Read the blog post again and answer the questions.**

1 How can we watch our health with connected clothing?
____
2 How does the denim jacket in the text play music?
____
3 What's good about creating electricity with clothes?
____
4 What does the blogger predict about 3-D printed clothes?
____

4 **Find words in the blog that mean:**

1 the part of clothing that covers your arm (A) ____
2 to move around something (B) ____
3 to put electricity into a device like a phone (C) ____
4 the latest information (D) ____
5 to produce something with a printer (D) ____

Voice it!

5 **Discuss the questions.**

1 Would you like to have any of the smart clothes in the blog?
2 What other things would you like clothes to do in the future?
3 Do you think smart clothes are important? Why / Why not?

Finished? p118 Ex 1

Watch video 1.2
How long has Tara been knitting?
How many people have bought Patrick's shoes?

LANGUAGE IN ACTION

Present perfect simple and present perfect continuous

Present perfect simple	Present perfect continuous
Scientists [1] ______ also **created** clothes with sensors.	Over the last few years, scientists [2] ______ **been developing** clothes which can record information.
He [3] ______ **bought** any 3-D printed clothing yet.	If you [4] ______ **been following** my updates on 3-D printing, check out these trendy designs.
[5] ______ you ever **seen** a jacket that can play music?	How long [6] ______ you **been reading** my blog?

1 **Complete the examples in the table above with the correct form of *have*.**

2 **Complete the rules with *simple* or *continuous*.**

1 In present perfect ______ sentences the focus is on the result of an activity.

2 In present perfect ______ sentences the focus is on how long the activity is.

3 **Put the words in the correct order to make sentences.**

1 lots of / I've / blog posts / written

I've written lots of blog posts.

2 since / a fashion blog / writing / She's been / January

______

3 made / Have you / your own clothes / ever / ?

______

4 been / He's / two years / designing / for / clothes

______

1.04 **4** **Complete the text with the present perfect continuous form of the verbs in the box. Listen and check.**

help make not practise ~~try~~ watch work

Recently I [1] 've been trying to learn how to knit. It's really difficult! I [2] ______ lots of videos online, but I [3] ______ very much. I [4] ______ a scarf for a few days now, but it's full of holes and looks awful. My mum [5] ______ me too, but she [6] ______ all week and hasn't really got much free time.

1.05 **5** **Complete the sentences with the present perfect simple or continous form of the verbs in brackets. Listen, check and repeat.**

1 How long has he been designing clothes? (design)

2 ______ you ever ______ to knit? (learn)

3 She ______ never ______ high-heeled shoes. (wear)

4 I ______ in these shoes all morning and my feet really hurt! (walk).

Use it!

6 **Imagine you are a fashion designer. Make questions with the present perfect simple or continuous. Then think of your answers.**

1 What / designed?

______

2 Who / worn your designs?

______

3 How long / designing clothes?

______

7 **Ask and answer the questions. Which designer makes the most interesting clothes? Why?**

I've designed a coat which changes colour when it gets wet!

Finished? p118 Ex 2

VOCABULARY AND LISTENING

Verbs related to clothes and shoes

1.06 **1 Read the fashion forum and match the verbs in bold with the definitions. Listen, check and repeat.**

ARE YOU A FOLLOWER OF FASHION?

MARIA I don't buy many clothes because they **go out of fashion** so quickly. I usually buy things that **go with** other clothes I already have. I like wearing green clothes because they **match** my eyes!

GISELA I'm really tall so it's difficult to find clothes that **fit** me, especially jeans! I wear jeans so much they **wear out**! Lots of clothes don't **suit** me, because they haven't been designed for tall people.

EDU I love fashion and I work in a clothes store on Saturdays. It's great because I get to try on loads of clothes. The worst part is the changing rooms. People leave clothes on the floor and I have to **hang up** the jackets and trousers and **fold** all the T-shirts. It takes forever!

IRINA Today I had a complete fashion disaster. I was trying on a dress in a shop. I managed to **do up** the zip! But when I tried to take the dress off I couldn't **undo** it. How embarrassing!

1 be the right size *fit*
2 not popular any longer ______
3 wear something so much it looks old ______
4 make someone look good ______
5 look good together ______
6 be similar or the same colour/type ______
7 close buttons or zips on clothes ______
8 open buttons or zips on clothes ______
9 put clothes on a coat hanger ______
10 bend clothes so that one part lies on another part ______

LEARN TO LEARN

Recording new verbs

Make sentences with new verbs so that you can remember how to use them.

2 Complete the sentences with the correct form of the verbs in the box and the words in brackets.

do up	hang up	not go with	suit	~~wear out~~

1 You never *wear out your shoes*. They always look new. (your shoes)
2 That colour ______. It looks good. (you)
3 This top ______. They're different styles. (my skirt)
4 ______ on your jacket. It's cold. (the zip)

Get it right!

The word *clothes* is always plural.

Your new clothes look great!

Use it!

3 Discuss the questions.

1 Which clothes fit you well?
2 Which ones suit you?
3 Which ones have you worn out?

An interview

1.07 **4 Listen to an interview with Carla. Where does she get her clothes from?**

1.07 **5 Listen again and complete the text.**

Carla started looking at fashion designs online when she was [1] *12*. She enjoys upcycling – creating [2] ______ from something that exists. She also decorates [3] ______ T-shirts and tops with her own designs. She knows that people buy fast fashion because the clothes are [4] ______ and that ethical fashion is [5] ______ than fast fashion but ethical fashion thinks about the people who [6] ______.

Pronunciation p141

LANGUAGE IN ACTION
Modifiers

Watch video 1.3
What are the top three fashion mistakes? What's the problem if your bedroom is totally messy?

I've been [1] _______ obsessed with fashion since I was a child.	**a** extremely / absolutely / _______ / really
They look [2] _______ good.	**b** quite / rather / fairly / _______
These clothes are [3] _______ more expensive …	**c** _______ / a little
but they last [4] _______ longer.	**d** _______ / far

1 **Complete the examples in the table above with *a bit*, *a lot*, *pretty* and *totally*. Use the same words in each line.**

2 **Which words (a–d) do we use before …**

1 comparative adjectives to show a big difference? _______
2 comparative adjectives to show a small difference? _______
3 strong adjectives? _______
4 adjectives to mean more than *a little* but less than *very*? _______

3 1.10 **Circle the correct words. Listen and check.**

Making materials like cotton or denim can be [1] *extremely* / *a lot* damaging for the environment. That's why it's [2] *absolutely* / *far* essential we create new materials from natural products that are [3] *fairly* / *a lot* better for the planet. Some materials like bamboo have been [4] *fairly* / *a little* successful. Others are still being developed, like a material from the rice plant, which is [5] *quite* / *a bit* similar to cotton, and one made from chicken feathers, which is [6] *pretty* / *a bit* warm, like wool. Technology has also made it [7] *really* / *far* easier to recycle materials like plastic bottles into clothes such as leggings and T-shirts, which is [8] *really* / *a lot* good news for the environment!

4 **Complete the sentences with the words in brackets.**

1 I feel __quite__ tired today. I need to sleep well otherwise I'll be __extremely__ tired tomorrow. (extremely / quite)
2 The shopping centre in our town is _______ good, but the one outside town is _______ better. (far / quite)
3 He creates _______ amazing designs, which are _______ more fun than ours. (a lot / totally)
4 I'm _______ good at art, but there are people in my class who are _______ more talented than me. (far / fairly)
5 This coat is _______ beautiful and it's only _______ more expensive than the other one. (a bit / absolutely)

Use it!

5 **Complete the sentences so they are true for you.**

1 I am pretty good at _______________.
2 I feel quite sad when _______________.
3 A subject I find a lot easier than before is _______________.
4 I'm a bit more interested in _______________ than before.
5 I think it's absolutely amazing that _______________.

6 **Guess what your partner wrote in their sentences. Score one point for each correct guess.**

Did you say, 'I am pretty good at English'?

No, I didn't. I said, 'I'm pretty good at art'.

Finished? p118 Ex 3

SPEAKING

Giving your opinion politely

1.11 **1 Listen to the conversation. Does Diego like the things?**

DIEGO Hey, Dana. How's it going?
DANA Hi Diego. I've been shopping all morning. I've bought some great stuff. Do you want to see?
DIEGO Yeah, sure.
DANA I got this striped jacket from Zaps, that new store they've just opened.
DIEGO Oh right. Wow! [1]That's … er … different!
DANA I know! It's totally out there!
DIEGO Mmm, [2] ________________ yellow and blue together, but the blue matches the colour of your eyes.
DANA Thanks! And check out these trousers.
DIEGO Flowery trousers! Wow! Very retro!
DANA I know! They fit really well. What do you think?
DIEGO Well, [3] ________________ , but I can see why you like them.
DANA Do you think they suit me?
DIEGO Yes, I guess so.
DANA I think I might wear them to go out later, with the jacket.
DIEGO Mmm, [4] ________________ I'd wear them together. [5] ________________ the trousers would go better with a plain top.
DANA No, patterns are totally in this year.
DIEGO You're such a fashion victim, Dana!

1.11 **2 Complete the conversation with the phrases from the *Useful language* box. Listen and check.**

Useful language

I don't know if …   I'm not a huge fan of …
I think maybe …   That's … er … different!
They're not exactly my style.

Watch video 1.4
Everyday English

check out   fashion victim   in   out there

3 Match the phrases in the *Everyday English* box with the words and phrases 1–4.

1 someone who follows fashion ____________
2 fashionable ____________
3 different ____________
4 look at ____________

PLAN

4 Write about the clothes in the photo:

What clothes are they?
Who bought them and why?
What do they look like?
Why do you like or not like them?

SPEAK

5 Practise the conversation with your partner. Remember to use the present perfect simple and continuous, modifiers, the vocabulary from this unit and phrases from the *Useful language* and *Everyday English* boxes.

CHECK

6 Work with another pair. Listen to their conversation and complete the notes.

Who bought them and why? ____________
____
What do they look like? ____________
____
Do the other pair like them? ____________
____

Na outra página: Leta se prepara para abrir a caixa. *No sentido horário, a partir do canto superior esquerdo*: de varinha na mão, Kama está em um monumento de um dos ancestrais de Leta; arte conceitual por Dermot Power e Hattie Story da elaborada caixa de ouro, com registros da família Lestrange; Leta senta sozinha no mausoléu dos Lestrange; arte por MinaLima da intrincada árvore genealógica dos Lestrange.

LEGADOS DE FAMÍLIA

Uma breve lição sobre o preconceito no Mundo Bruxo: a essência das ideias de Grindelwald está na crença na supremacia dos bruxos de sangue-puro, dos quais a dinastia dos Lestrange é representante.

Mas nem todas as famílias de sangue-puro são tão puras quanto parecem. A árvore genealógica dos Lestrange será um dos pontos principais da história, roubada da Sala de Registros do Ministério da Magia Francês. Quando a caixa for aberta, a linhagem da família puro-sangue será totalmente revelada em três dimensões.

"Nós planejamos de forma simples e, no processo, incrementamos em 3D", conta o designer gráfico Eduardo Lima.

"Foi interessante, do ponto de vista conceitual", diz Miraphora Mina. "Rowling disse o que acontece no diálogo, mas nós não conhecíamos toda a história por trás disso. Como na árvore genealógica da família Black em Harry Potter, tivemos que pedir a ela a linhagem real. Ela acabou nos dando apenas um lado da árvore Lestrange, então eu tive que produzir o outro lado. É bem complexo. Você tem que ter muito cuidado sobre como eles estão todos relacionados."

"Todos eles acabaram se casando com seus primos", ri Lima.

"A árvore tem uma estética parecida com o estilo de Hieronymus Bosch", diz Mina, referindo-se ao pinto holandês do século XV, famoso por representações humanas com rostos distorcidos pelo pecado.

"Mal posso esperar para ver isso em 3D", diz ela.

um guarda-roupa habitado por um Bicho-papão são exemplos disso.

O que realmente inspira Pinnock é que, embora este mundo extraordinário criado por J. K. Rowling seja completamente mágico, ele também é um pano de fundo dos anos vinte do mundo real. Ela e sua equipe devem ter analisado milhares de fotografias da época. A pesquisa também tem sido crucial para "dar um ponto de partida consciente" de determinado período.

E o mais legal é que Paris ampliou as possibilidades, especialmente com a inclusão de um circo mágico. Em comparação, Nova York era quase escura e opressiva. "Mais *steampunk*, suponho", ela reflete. "Também foi um local incrível no qual pudemos criar nossas sutis reviravoltas mágicas."

Há muito mais magia no novo filme, e ela achou isso muito libertador. "Realmente podemos levar isso ao extremo."

Trabalhando em parceria com o time de criação de adereços, dirigido por Pierre Bohanna, muitos dos itens mágicos que preenchem as cenas são construídos precisamente para a ocasião.

Há também os diversos itens comprados em bazares, feiras e mercados. Postes de luz recuperados, móveis de rua e bolas de cristal importadas da China. "Ganhamos cerca de seis meses", ela explica, "o que é bem corrido, e fomos a uma quantidade incrível de mercados e feiras na área de Paris. Arranjamos alguns caminhões e compramos tudo isso antes mesmo de termos um roteiro."

Era o caso de olhar para sua própria bola de cristal e pensar "o que poderia funcionar" ou "eu poderia pintar isso."

A equipe de Pinnock levou cinco dias para decorar o sótão da meio-elfa Irma Dugard na rua Philippe Lorand, para onde Credence vai em sua busca pela mãe. "Quando a atriz francesa que interpreta Irma entrou, ela se jogou na cama, um pouco parecida com uma criança quando ama um lugar. Ela exclamou: 'Isso é tão francês. Eu simplesmente sinto que estou na França.'"

Da esquerda para a direita: A elegância do Ministério da Magia Francês foi alcançada graças à visão genial de Stuart Craig e à precisão da equipe de cenografia de Pinnock; roupas de borracha protetoras de Newt e Bunty, penduradas na parede do porão; uma bruxa aparece com um dos fantásticos moldes; *(na página)* embora seja improvável que seja visto na câmera, este calendário de Newt foi cuidadosamente preenchido com adereços de papel que revelam a vida do mago.

Four steps

to reduce your fashion footprint

Here are some ideas you can try!

- Have a clothes swap party. Swap clothes you don't want with your friends.
- Save energy. Wash clothes less often, dry clothes naturally, don't iron!
- Give old clothes to second-hand shops. Don't throw them away!
- Buy fewer, better quality new clothes.

Comments

Great post! It got me thinking about how to reduce my fashion footprint. I talked to my parents and we decided to try and reduce the amount of energy we use on our clothes. Usually we wash all our clothes every time we wear them, even when they're still pretty clean, but this month we've been washing clothes less often, and we haven't ironed anything. My parents have saved money and I've been much better at hanging up my clothes! **Carlos**

Thanks for sharing! I had no idea that I throw so many clothes away! I had a clothes swap party last week. I got a great denim jacket that I absolutely love! I also got two long-sleeved tops and some cool high-heeled boots for free! I was absolutely amazed that we swapped everything! Since reading your post I've decided to buy far fewer new clothes in the future. **Amie**

WRITING

A blog comment

1 **Look at the blog post. How can people reduce their fashion footprint?**

2 **Read the blog comments. Answer the questions.**

1 Were the ideas that Carlos and Amie tried successful? How do you know?

____

2 What does Amie want to do in the future?

____

3 **Find the phrases from the *Useful language* box in the blog comments. Which phrases can you use when you …**

1 enjoy reading a post?

____

2 learn something new from the post?

____

3 change your behaviour because of the post?

____

Useful language

Great post!	We decided to …
I had no idea that …	Since reading your post I've …
It got me thinking about …	Thanks for sharing!

Write your own blog comment.

PLAN

4 **Look at the ideas in the blog post and make notes about which one to write about.**

Which ideas will you try out? ______________________________

Do you think it will go well? Why? / Why not?

____

What other ideas would you like to try in the future? ______________________________

WRITE

5 **Write your blog comment. Remember to include the present perfect simple and continuous, modifiers, vocabulary from this unit and phrases from the *Useful language* box.**

CHECK

6 **Do you …**

- explain why an idea might or might not work well?
- explain what you would like to try in the future?

Finished? p118 Ex 4

AROUND THE WORLD

Globetrotters
Watch video 1.5
What we wear and why

- Why do we wear clothes and what do they show about us?
- What is a *deel* and why do Mongolian people wear it?
- What do the colours blue, white, green, yellow and orange represent for the Masai people?

READING
A travel guide

1.12 **1 Are the sentences about the kilt true or false? Read the travel guide and check your answers.**

1. Kilts are only worn by men. ________
2. Kilts have not always been made of tartan. ________
3. Tartans today indicate where people live. ________
4. Scottish dress is different for men and women. ________
5. Tartan patterns are popular outside Scotland. ________

Traditional Scottish dress

You have probably seen photos of Scotland's most famous piece of clothing, the kilt. But did you know that Scottish men have been wearing kilts for centuries? A kilt used to be an extremely long piece of heavy plain or checked material that men from the Scottish Highlands wore every day. They wrapped the material around their waist and over one shoulder or their head to protect them from the cold wind or rain. Nowadays, the design of the kilt is totally different. It is knee-length and made from wool, with a pattern of vertical and horizontal stripes in different colours called tartan. Tartan designs used to indicate the area where people lived and were far less colourful than they are today. Since the 18th century, people have been wearing tartan designs that represent their family name or clan (group of families) and today there are over 4,500 designs! The kilt forms part of the traditional Highland dress, which is quite different for men and women.

MEN:
- tartan kilt and a kilt pin
- leather belt
- sporran – a small leather or fur bag that hangs from the belt. There are no pockets in a kilt!
- plain or tartan socks
- kilt knife – a small knife kept in one sock
- ghillies – plain, flat leather shoes with long laces

WOMEN:
- long or knee-length tartan kilt
- tartan shawl – a piece of material worn over your shoulders
- plain or tartan socks
- ghillies

2 **Use the travel guide to complete the table.**

Kilts in the 18th century	Kilts in the 21st century
One long piece of cloth worn around waist and over shoulder	
Highland dress for men	**Highland dress for women**
Who wears traditional tartan clothes?	**Who wears modern tartan clothes?**

Highland dress is extremely popular in Scotland for special occasions such as weddings, funerals or parties, particularly for men. Women often wear kilts to do traditional Scottish dancing at sports and cultural events. Nowadays, tartan isn't just used for traditional dress in Scotland. Fashion designers around the world use tartan to create modern designs such as tartan trousers or tartan shoes and celebrities from Rihanna to Shawn Mendes have been photographed wearing tartan. Even though people have worn tartan for centuries, it is still popular today and looks like it's not going to go out of fashion any time soon.

3 **Find the nouns and match them with the definitions.**

dress funeral laces pin shawl

1 a ceremony when a person dies ______
2 a combination of clothes worn together for a particular situation ______
3 a small piece of metal to attach clothes ______
4 a large piece of cloth worn over your shoulders or head ______
5 string used to fasten shoes ______

LEARN TO LEARN

Using spidergrams

Spidergrams can help you remember words that have a link with other words.

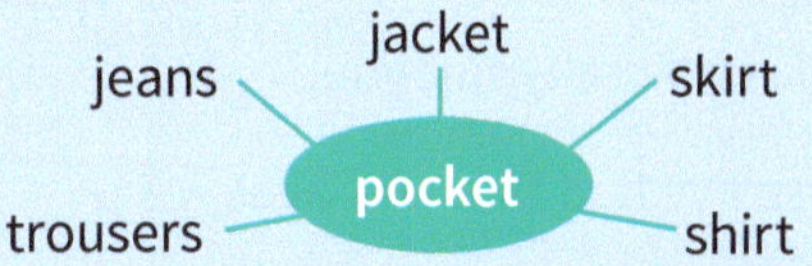

4 **Make a spidergram of clothes and shoes which have laces, a zip, buttons or sleeves.**

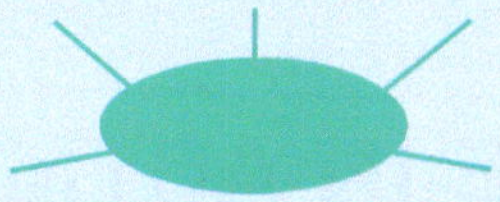

5 **Which words did you both write? Add any new words to your spidergrams.**

Voice it!

6 **Discuss the questions.**

1 What is traditional dress in your country?
2 When do people wear it?

Explore it!

Guess the correct answer.

It was illegal to wear tartan in the middle of the 18th century in Scotland. True or false?

a true b false

Find another fact about traditional Scottish dress. Write a question for your partner to answer.

OWN IT! The Culture Project Teacher's Resource Bank

1 REVIEW

VOCABULARY

1 Circle the odd word out.

1	baggy	tight	spotted
2	cotton	long-sleeved	denim
3	flowery	flat	plain
4	cotton	striped	checked
5	plain	flat	high-heeled

2 Match 1–5 with a–e.

1 **Hang up** your clothes, ☐
2 I can't **undo** my jacket, ☐
3 These jeans are **worn out** ☐
4 This T-shirt **doesn't fit** me any more, ☐
5 Your glasses really **suit** you, ☐

a because I've had them for ages.
b it's too small.
c the zip's broken.
d they look great!
e they're all over the floor.

LANGUAGE IN ACTION

3 Complete the text with the present perfect simple or continuous form of the verbs in brackets.

16-year-old Moziah Bridges [1]________ (design) ties since he was nine. His grandmother taught him to make bow ties and since then he [2]________ (own) his own business. The designer [3]________ (appear) in magazines and on TV and [4]________ (make) a collection of ties for basketball teams in the USA. Mo is still at school but [5]________ (work) in the evenings. It [6]________ (not be) easy, but his mum helps him and he [7]________ (employ) more people as his business [8]________ (grow). Mo often gives talks to other people who [9]________ (think) about starting a business.

4 Circle the correct modifier to complete the sentences.

1 It takes *a little / quite* longer to fold your clothes, but then you don't have to iron them.
2 Where did you get that jacket? I *far / absolutely* love it!
3 The second film in the series was *a bit / pretty* better than the first one, but not much.
4 I speak *a lot / fairly* good Chinese, but I can't write it.
5 I'm *far / totally* confused by his explanation. I don't understand it at all.
6 Have you seen this video? It's *really / a lot* funny.
7 That T-shirt is *far / really* nicer than the other one, but it's *quite / a lot* expensive.

Self-assessment

I can use words to describe clothes and shoes.

I can use verbs to talk about clothes and shoes.

I can use the *present perfect simple* and *present perfect continuous*.

I can use modifiers.

LEARN TO LEARN

LEARN TO ... WRITE DIFFERENT KINDS OF EXAMPLE SENTENCES

You can write different kinds of example sentences to help you understand and remember new words.

1 Read Ela's blog. Why does she recommend using the different kinds of example sentences to remember new words?

Ela's English learning BLOG

Today's tip: example sentences

Hi everyone! Today we're looking at a great way to learn vocabulary: example sentences. When I learn new words, I often use them in sentences to help me learn and remember them. There are different types of example sentences you can use. They're all good for different reasons.

a sentences about you, your family or your friends – when you use words in sentences about things people you know have done, the words are easier to remember

b funny sentences – a funny image can help the word stay in your memory

c sentences that explain the word – these make the meaning clear, like the examples in dictionaries

Here are some of my latest examples. Can you guess which types they are?

1 I prefer **plain** T-shirts to ones with writing or pictures on them.

2 Your skin gets **sweaty** when you're hot or exercise a lot.

3 My baby brother always wipes his nose on his **sleeve**.

4 The giraffe couldn't **do up** the zip on his jacket because it was too long!

5 A **checked** pattern is a pattern of squares of different colours.

6 I thought I saw a zebra – but it was a horse in a black and white **striped** T-shirt.

So ... that's all from me today. Don't forget to share some example sentences of your own. You can post them below!

2 Match Ela's examples 1–6 with types a–c.

1 ______ 4 ______
2 ______ 5 ______
3 ______ 6 ______

OWN IT!

3 Choose five words from the box and write an example sentence for each one. Use all of Ela's types a–c at least once.

baggy	charge	fashion victim	flat	hang up	high-heeled	laces	not go with	spotted	updates

1 ______
2 ______
3 ______
4 ______
5 ______

4 Tell your partner your sentences from Exercise 3. Which types a–c are they? Which sentences are your favourites and why?

2 CHANGES

LEARNING OUTCOMES

I can ...

- understand texts about international exchanges and a mystery object
- explain how to use something
- write an opinion essay
- understand how to use *used to* and *would* for past habits, the past simple, and the past perfect with *never, already, by (then), by the time*
- talk about changes and parts of objects
- practise learning new words by using them in different situations and identifying key words to understand audio texts
- make a history exhibition.

Start it!

1 Look at the photo. Do you know what this animal is, and how it changes?
2 Before you watch, how do you think cities change over time?
3 Which two events changed the city of Seoul? Watch and check.
4 How has your town or city changed?

Watch video 2.1

p25

Language in action 2.2

p27

Language in action 2.3

p28

Everyday English 2.4

VOCABULARY
Phrasal verbs: changes

1 **Which of the phrases a–l describes picture 1? Which phrase describes picture 2?**

a **settle down** in a new school
b **look forward to** the weekend
c **sign up** for French lessons
d **try out** a new restaurant
e **turn out** well
f **move out** of a house
g **move to** a new school
h **go back** to the beginning
i **end up** in the wrong place
j **go through** a hard time
k **do without** the Internet
l **turn down** an invitation

1

2

2 2.01 **Match definitions 1–12 with the phrasal verbs a–l in Exercise 1. Listen, check and repeat.**

1 feel happy about something in the future b
2 not have something
3 finally be in a place/situation
4 experience
5 stop living in a particular place
6 try something new
7 start to feel happy in a new place/situation
8 return
9 join an organised activity
10 say no to something
11 have a particular result
12 change to

3 2.02 **Listen to six conversations and complete the sentences using the phrases in Exercise 1.**

1 Mr Smith decides to ________________ for French classes.
2 Molly ________________ the baseball game. Ben ________________ to the game.
3 Tom is ________________ at the moment. He ________________ new school.
4 Jo asks Ed to ________________ the beginning.
5 The girls are going to ________________ restaurant.
6 In the end, Leila's party ________________.

LEARN TO LEARN
Using words in different situations

Using new words in different situations helps you to remember them.

4 **Think of different situations for the phrasal verbs in Exercise 1.**

What can you look forward to?

A party … the end of exams …

Use it!

5 **Think of questions using the phrasal verbs in Exercise 1. Ask and answer.**

Have you tried out a new restaurant recently?

Yes. We went to a great Italian restaurant last week.

Explore it!

Guess the correct answer.

Where do most international students come from?

a USA b China c India

Find out a fact about students in your country. Write a question for your partner.

ACE EXCHANGES – DISCOVER A NEW WORLD AND A NEW YOU!

Student testimonials

LUCY

I love school here – it's so different to the USA. Students have almost no homework and very few exams. At my school, we don't even have school subjects. We study topics and do projects instead. It's a great way to learn.

This experience has really helped me to become more confident. I didn't use to be adventurous, but I've tried lots of new things since I arrived here eight months ago. For example, I went on a reindeer safari on my birthday, and I've been going ice-swimming every Saturday. Plus, I've made lots of friends. Finns are very cool people.

It hasn't all been easy. Winter is very hard because it's really dark – there are only three or four hours of light every day. The good thing is that you can see the beautiful Northern Lights.

If you get the opportunity to study abroad don't turn it down, especially not if you can come to Finland!

BEN

Last year I spent six wonderful months in Mexico. I used to dream about living in a different country, so when I discovered Ace Exchanges I signed up immediately. It was an absolutely incredible experience. I loved the mix of local, European and African cultures, and the people were really outgoing.

Of course, I went through some ups and downs at first, especially dealing with a different school system. For example, many Mexican schools have two timetables. Some students start school at 7.30 am and some – like me – start at 2 pm. We would finish at 8 pm! Also, I didn't speak much Spanish when I arrived, so it was quite difficult to follow lessons. But my classmates would always help me, and I improved a lot.

I felt a bit homesick from time to time, but now I feel like I have two homes. In fact, I've decided to go to university there. I'm really looking forward to going back.

READING

A brochure

1 **Look at the photos. Which show Finland? Which show Mexico? What do you think it is like to live there?**

2.03 **2** **Read the brochure. Write *L* (Lucy) or *B* (Ben).**

Which person …

1. has been abroad for more than half a year? ___
2. found the country's education system difficult? ___
3. has changed in a positive way? ___
4. found part of the year difficult because of the light? ___
5. likes the variety of cultures? ___
6. can do something better than they used to do? ___

3 **Find words in the brochure that mean:**

1. happy to try new things (Lucy) ________
2. from the nearby area (Ben) ________
3. friendly and sociable (Ben) ________
4. a mix of good and bad experiences (Ben) ________
5. missing your family (Ben) ________

4 **Read the sentences and write *T* (true), *F* (false) or *DS* (doesn't say).**

1. In Finland, students never do exams. F
2. Students have long breaks in Finland. ___
3. Lucy has been ice-swimming more than once. ___
4. Ben never wanted to leave the USA. ___
5. Mexican students don't all finish school at the same time. ___
6. Ben wants to go back home soon. ___

Voice it!

5 **Discuss the questions.**

1. Can you think of a country you would like to go on an exchange to?
2. Why would you like to visit that country?
3. What do you think would be difficult about living there?

Finished? p119 Ex 1

LANGUAGE IN ACTION

used to, *would* and past simple

Watch video 2.2
What did her grandmother use to write on?
What did she use to do outdoors?

used to / would	Past simple
I [1] ________ **to** dream about living in a different country.	I **went** on a reindeer safari.
I **didn't** [2] ________ **to** be adventurous.	I **didn't speak** much Spanish.
Did Lucy [3] ________ **to** be adventurous?	**Did** Ben **learn** a lot of Spanish?
My classmates [4] ________ always help me.	

Pronunciation p141

1 Complete the examples in the table above with one word in each gap. Use the brochure on page 24 to help you.

2 Complete the rules with *used to*/*would* or the past simple.

1 We use ____________ to talk about situations that continued and actions that happened more than once in the past.

2 We use ____________ to talk about things that happened only once.

3 Complete the text with *used to* and the verbs in brackets.

My grandfather's childhood was different to mine. When he was a boy, he never [1] used to have (have) many toys, but he [2] ____________ (have) a lot of time. He [3] ____________ (love) playing outside. Sometimes, his friends [4] ____________ (play) outside all day – they [5] ____________ (go) out early and then they [6] ____________ (come) home late at night. I think it [7] ____________ (be) safer for children then.

Get it right!

We don't use *would* with past situations, only repeated actions.

We used to live in Murcia.

NOT ~~*We would live in Murcia.*~~

We used to / would play tennis at school.

4 Circle the correct words. Sometimes both are possible.

1 More people *would* / *used to* live in the countryside than in cities. Now it's the opposite.

2 In the past, TV channels *would* / *used to* stop at night.

3 Some people *didn't use to* / *wouldn't* smile in photos because their teeth were bad.

4 Many people *would* / *used to* think that the Earth was flat.

5 Complete the sentences with *used to*, *didn't use to* or the past simple and the verbs in brackets.

1 For his birthday, Aidan got (get) a new bike. He loved it.

2 Ada ____________ (like) apples much, but now she does.

3 I ____________ (end up) in the wrong place yesterday because I didn't have a map.

4 When Bill was younger, he ____________ (turn down) invitations all the time because he was so shy.

Use it!

6 Write questions for a partner about their parents' lives with *used to* or the past simple.

1 what toys / play with ________________________

2 study English / at school ________________________

3 how / meet ________________________

7 Ask and answer the questions.

What toys did your parents use to play with?

I think they used to play with wooden toys, and they would often play outside.

Finished? p119 Ex 2

VOCABULARY AND LISTENING

Parts of objects

1 **Look at the photos. Which objects do you recognise?**

2.08 **2** **Match the words in the box with parts of the objects 1–10. Listen, check and repeat.**

button		cable		cover		display		handle	
key		lens	1	lid		plug		strap	

2.09 **3** **Circle the correct words. Listen and check.**

1 When you carry a backpack, do you use one *strap* / *cable* or both? Why?

2 Do you always put the *handle* / *lid* back on the toothpaste after using it?

3 How often do you clean the *key* / *lens* of the camera on your phone?

4 Without looking, can you remember what is on the *cover* / *display* of this book?

5 Can you name six objects that have an on/off *plug* / *button*?

6 Do you take your phone charger *cable* / *display* with you when you go out?

Use it!

4 **Ask and answer the questions in Exercise 3. Are your answers similar or different?**

A quiz show

2.10 **5** **Listen to a quiz show about retro objects. Which three objects in Exercise 1 are mentioned?**

LEARN TO LEARN

Identifying key words

Identifying key words before you listen can help you understand what you hear.

6 **Read the questions and the options and underline the key words.**

1 Joey pushes the buzzer too early because he …
   a can't wait to play.
   b doesn't understand the rules.

2 Nicola guesses the first object correctly because she …
   a has seen one before.
   b has heard of it before.

3 People had fax machines …
   a in their houses.
   b in their workplaces.

4 People used lava lamps …
   a instead of lightbulbs.
   b because they were attractive.

2.10 **7** **Listen again and answer the questions in Exercise 6.**

Voice it!

8 **Discuss the questions.**

1 Do you know any retro objects that have come back into fashion?

2 What do you think of them?

LANGUAGE IN ACTION

Past perfect with *never, already, by (then), by the time*

Watch video 2.3
Where did she go last week?
When were 3-D printers first developed?

This was before anyone **had** [1] ________ **heard** of printers. I**'d heard** of fax machines before, but I**'d** [2] ________ **seen** one. They**'d** [3] ________ **gone** out of fashion **by the time** you were born.
I **hadn't started** yet.
Had you [4] ________ **seen** a digital watch before then?

1 **Complete the examples in the table above with *already*, *ever* or *never*.**

2 **Circle the correct words to complete the rules.**

1. *Already*, *never* and *ever* come *before* / *after* the main verb.
2. *By the time* means *before* / *after* something happened.

3 **Answer the questions with the past perfect.**

1. How did you know what would happen in the film? (already / read / the book)
   Because I had already read the book.
2. Why did you get lost? (never / be / there before)
   ____
3. Did you get a ticket for the concert? No, (by the time / I went online / they / sell out)
   ____
4. How was the party? (already / finish / when we got there)
   ____

2.11 **4** **Complete the text with the past simple or the past perfect. Listen and check.**

Last year I [1] went (go) on an exchange to Moscow. I [2] ________ (never / travel) alone before, so I [3] ________ (feel) nervous at first. Before I [4] ________ (go), I [5] ________ (already / learn) to read the Russian alphabet, although I [6] ________ (not practise) speaking Russian. By the time I [7] ________ (leave), I [8] ________ (improve) a lot. Everybody in Moscow [9] ________ (be) really kind and friendly, but it [10] ________ (not be) easy to deal with the cold weather. I [11] ________ (not pack) enough warm clothes, so I had to buy some after I [12] ________ (arrive). Anyway, I can't wait to go back. I [13] ________ (not expect) to enjoy it much before I actually [14] ________ (get) there, but in the end I really [15] ________ (do)!

Use it!

5 **Ask and answer the questions about the topics below. Use the past perfect.**

1. hear of / connected clothing?
2. see / a picture of 3-D printed clothes?
3. hear of / ice-swimming?
4. see / a picture of the Northern Lights?

Before you started using this book, had you ever heard of connected clothing?

No, I'd never heard of it, but now I want to know more! / Yes, I had. I'd already read about it online.

Finished? p119 Ex 3

SPEAKING

Explaining how to use something

1 (2.12) **Listen to the conversation. Which of the things in the box does the typewriter have?**

cable display ink keys plug speaker

YUSUF What's that? [1] Is it some kind of computer?
MERI No, it's my grandad's old typewriter.
YUSUF Where's the display?
MERI There isn't one, and there's no plug or cable.
YUSUF That's so old-school! How did it work?
MERI The paper would move as you typed. [2] ________ press the keys hard, but not too fast or they get stuck. Try it out!
YUSUF [3] ________
MERI That's it. Just imagine – people used to type books on these things!
YUSUF No way! I can't even find the letters I want.
MERI You need to sign up for typing classes! They're in the same place as an ordinary keyboard.
YUSUF Oh no! [4] ________ How do I go back? There's no 'delete' key.
MERI [5] ________ start all over again.
YUSUF No, thanks! Anyway, how come your grandad had this?
MERI He used to need it for work, but after a while he ended up buying a computer.
YUSUF I'm not surprised! I'm glad they'd invented computers by the time I started school! I'd hate to do my homework on this!

2 (2.12) **Complete the conversation with the phrases from the *Useful language* box. Listen and check.**

Useful language

Is it some kind of …? I've messed it up.
Like this, you mean? What you do is, you …
You'll have to …

Watch video 2.4
Everyday English

all over again
I'm not surprised.
old-school That's it.

3 **Complete the sentences with the phrases in the *Everyday English* box.**

1 Barry's not here yet. ________ – he's always late.
2 A Do I press this button here?
B ________
3 Your new jacket's so ________. My dad used to have one like that.
4 Oh no! I've lost my homework! I'll have to do it ________.

PLAN

4 **Choose one of the objects on page 26. Make notes on how to use it.**

SPEAK

5 **Practise the explanation with your partner. Remember to use past tenses, vocabulary from this unit and phrases from the *Useful language* and *Everyday English* boxes.**

CHECK

6 **Work with another pair. Listen to their explanation and complete the notes.**

How does the object work? ________

____

Do you understand how to use it? ________

____

WRITING

An opinion essay

1 In what ways has life changed for teenagers in the last 30 years?

2 Read the essay. Does it mention any of your ideas in Exercise 1?

Are teenagers today more or less stressed than previous generations?

The world has changed a great deal in the last few decades, especially for teenagers, and not always in a positive way. In particular, people of my generation are a lot more stressed than teenagers in the past.

Firstly, we are under enormous pressure to do well in exams. This means that we spend a lot of time studying. Young people didn't use to study as much because it wasn't always necessary to go to university. Therefore, they had more time to relax and hang out with friends.

Secondly, previous generations didn't have online profiles to worry about. In fact, young people 20 or 30 years ago hadn't even heard of 'followers' and 'likes' because social media hadn't been invented yet. For people of my age, it is almost impossible to do without social media. In addition, it can become extremely addictive.

In conclusion, I would say that teenagers today have more stressful lives than our parents did.

3 **Complete the table with the linkers from the *Useful language* box. Look at the linkers in the essay to help you.**

Order of ideas	Connection between ideas
firstly	

Useful language

firstly in addition in conclusion secondly therefore this means that

4 **Complete the essay with the linkers from the *Useful language* box. Do you agree with the writer? Sometimes there is more than one possible answer.**

Some people think that online games are worse for you than traditional games, because they are addictive and don't involve physical exercise, but is this always true?

In my opinion, online games have many good points. [1]Firstly, they improve your memory and your problem-solving skills.

[2]________, you can make friends. [3]________, you play with people from around the world. [4]________ you often have to communicate in English and [5]________ your English improves. However, it's important to spend time with your friends offline.

[6]________, online games can be unhealthy, but only if you spend all your time playing them.

Write an opinion essay.

PLAN

5 **Look at the statement and make notes.**

Teenagers today have more freedom than in the past.

Do you agree or disagree with the statement?

Write two reasons for your opinion.

Give a summary of your opinion.

WRITE

6 **Write your opinion essay. Remember to include, *used to*, the past simple and past perfect and phrases from the *Useful language* box.**

CHECK

7 **Do you ...**

- give your opinion?
- give reasons for your opinion?
- summarise your opinion?

Finished? p119 Ex 4

THE HISTORY PROJECT

1 FASHION

Fashion is always changing, and old styles often come back into fashion, although few people look forward to seeing 1970s fashion again. If you watch TV shows from that decade, you will see that people used to wear trousers that were tight at the top and wide at the bottom, flowery dresses, a lot of tight cotton T-shirts or shirts with big collars, and plenty of big round glasses. During the early 1970s, bright colours were extremely trendy, but by the end of the decade they had almost completely disappeared. Black, white, grey and brown had replaced them, although people still wore enormous glasses.

2 TECHNOLOGY

It is hard to imagine dealing with the ups and downs of modern life without computers and smartphones. However, in the 70s there were very few computers, and the ones that existed were a lot bigger than those we have today. They were far slower, with simple displays and enormous buttons. Compared to the devices we use today, they also had very little memory. In fact, the computers on the Apollo spaceships that took men to the moon had less memory than some modern toasters. By the beginning of the 1970s, some companies had started to use computers in their offices, but it was extremely rare to see a computer in a house. In fact, most people had never used one, and some people had never seen one.

A retro museum exhibition

1 **Look at the photos. What period in history do you think they are from?**

2.13 2 **Read the exhibit labels. Which one do you find most interesting? Why?**

3 **Complete the table about exhibits 2 and 3.**

	1	2	3
Area	fashion	technology	music
Period	1970s		
Examples	trousers (tight at top, baggy at bottom), flowery dresses, big glasses, bright colours		
Changes over time	black, white, grey, brown became more popular		

3 MUSIC

Music has always been an important part of teenage identity, but in an age of streaming and downloading it's easy to forget that it hasn't always been as available as it is today. In the 1970s young music fans would spend hours in record shops looking for new music to buy. It wasn't only the music that was popular. The record covers were also important, and many of them became famous for their artwork. By the middle of the 1990s, CDs had become more popular than records. Nevertheless, people continued to collect records and DJs still used to play them at discos. Recently, they have come back into fashion, as many people prefer the sound of a record to the sound of a digital file.

How to schedule

4 Ask your teacher how long you have to complete the project. Then decide together how long to spend on each of these stages:

1. looking for information and photos
2. writing draft texts for the labels
3. checking and correcting the drafts
4. writing the final labels and putting them on a poster with the photos.

PLAN

5 Work in groups. Complete the steps below.

- Decide which period in history you want to concentrate on (for example, the 19th century, the 1980s).
- Choose three areas you want to focus on.

entertainment	fashion	food and drink
house and home	school life	
technology/communication	toys and games	

- Decide who is going to research and write about which exhibit.

PRESENT

6 Present your history exhibition on the wall of your classroom. Remember to include a title for each label, vocabulary from this unit, *used to*, the past simple and past perfect and the tips in *How to* schedule.

CHECK

7 Read the other groups' history exhibitions. What areas are they focusing on? Which group's exhibition is most interesting?

2 REVIEW

VOCABULARY

1 Complete the conversation with the correct form of a phrasal verb.

A How was your bike trip? Where did you go?

B Well, we wanted to [1] ________ a new route. We were planning to cycle to this old village near the sea, but we got lost and [2] ________ on a farm!

A Didn't you have a map with you?

B No, but the farmer helped us, so it [3] ________ OK in the end. We found the village!

A Was it nice there?

B Beautiful. I'd love to [4] ________ one day. How was your weekend?

A Not great. I was sick. My friends wanted me to go a concert. I'd said yes, and I [5] ________ to it, but in the end I had to [6] ________ them ________ .

2 Circle the correct words.

Did you know ... ?

- The [1]*lids / covers* of plastic water bottles are made from a different plastic to the bottle.
- If you change the [2]*lens / display* on your phone to black and white, it can become less addictive.
- On old trains, you couldn't open the doors with a [3]*button / plug*. You had to use a [4]*strap / handle*, like a normal door.
- Every second, 600,000 people around the world press the space [5]*cable / key* when they're on a computer.

LANGUAGE IN ACTION

3 Complete the text with *used to*, *would* or the past simple and the verb in brackets. Sometimes there is more than one possible answer.

My dad's a writer now, although he [1] ________ (not be). He [2] ________ (be) a diplomat, so when I was small, my family [3] ________ (move) countries all the time. Once, we [4] ________ (live) in three different countries in two years! I remember when I [5] ________ (move) to the school where I am now, in Rio de Janeiro. I [6] ________ (not know) any Portuguese at first, so the first week [7] ________ (be) difficult. I used to take my lunch to the playground and then I [8] ________ (eat) it alone. However, Brazilian people are really friendly, so after a few days my classmates [9] ________ (start) to invite me to eat with them and I quickly [10] ________ (make) lots of friends. We've been living here for many years now, and I'm really happy.

4 Complete Ben's message to Tom with the past perfect.

Tom, I'm so sorry I missed the wedding! I decided to take the car to the airport, but because I [1] ________ (never / drive) there before, I got lost. Just the night before, I [2] ________ (think), 'I must fix the GPS!', but then I completely forgot! Anyway, I got to the airport around two o'clock. The plane [3] ________ (not taken off), but by the time I finished checking in, the gate [4] ________ (close). I tried to buy a ticket for the next flight, but they [5] ________ (already / sell out)!

Self-assessment

- I can use phrasal verbs to talk about changes.
- I can use words to talk about parts of objects.
- I can use *used to*, *would* and the past simple.
- I can use the past perfect with *never*, *already*, *by (then)*, *by the time*.

LEARN TO … HELP YOUR PARTNER IMPROVE THEIR WRITING

When you write something, ask your partner to check it. You can improve your writing this way.

1 Read the instructions for the writing task. Correct Edison's mistakes to help him improve.

WRITING TASK

Write about a favourite toy or game from your childhood.

- Write between 100 and 130 words.
- Use language from this unit.

Don't forget to use punctuation and check your spelling!

When I was little, I [1] ~~use~~ used to play with Lego® bricks all the time. I would [2] building ________ all kinds of things – cars, [3] airplaynes ________, houses. I even built a computer with keys and a display. After I finished one thing, I would keep it and then try out something else, but I once [4] used to build ________ a ship that I kept for weeks. [5] I've ________ never built anything like it before. However, I remember my mum [6] would be ________ really angry with me one day because I played with it in the bathroom and ended up damaging the sides of the bath. I've still got a photo of it somewhere [7] ________

Number of words: 107

2 Answer the questions in the checklist. Has Edison completed the task in Exercise 1?

Checklist		
	Edison's writing	**W**
Has he/she …		
1 written about the topic?	Yes / No	Yes / No
2 written between 100 and 130 words?	Yes / No	Yes / No
3 used phrasal verbs for changes and words for parts of objects?	Yes / No	Yes / No
4 added details to make it interesting?	Yes / No	Yes / No
How well has he/she used …		
5 the past simple?	☹ 😐 ☺	☹ 😐 ☺
6 *used to* and *would*?	☹ 😐 ☺	☹ 😐 ☺
7 the past perfect?	☹ 😐 ☺	☹ 😐 ☺
8 punctuation?	☹ 😐 ☺	☹ 😐 ☺
9 correct spelling?	☹ 😐 ☺	☹ 😐 ☺
Other comments?	*I enjoyed the part about your mum being angry!*	

OWN IT!

3 Do the writing task in Exercise 1.

4 Answer the questions in the checklist for your partner's writing.

5 Tell your partner what you like and what they can improve.

3 FOOD FOR THOUGHT

LEARNING OUTCOMES

I can ...

- understand texts from an online forum and a cooking show
- give cooking instructions
- write a listicle
- understand how to use different future forms
- talk about cooking and quantities
- make adjectives from verbs, use diagrams, and understand words from context by using the rest of the text.

Start it!

1. Look at the photo. Would you like to eat this food? Why? / Why not?
2. Before you watch, how do you think food has changed in the last 100 years?
3. What two foods will we eat more of in the future? Watch and check.
4. Are there other ways that our eating habits may change in the future?

Watch video 3.1

p37

Language in action 3.2

p39

Language in action 3.3

p40

Everyday English 3.4

p42

Globetrotters 3.5

VOCABULARY

Cooking verbs

3.01 **1 Match the verbs in the box with photos 1–12. Listen, check and repeat.**

bake	☐	chop	☐	fry	☐
grate	☐	grill	☐	heat	☐
overcook	☐	peel	☐	roast	☐
season	☐	slice	☐	spread	☐

3.02 **2 Circle the correct verbs to complete the instructions to make a homemade pizza. Listen and check.**

[1]*Spread* / *Peel* the tomatoes and [2]*chop* / *overcook* them. Then [3]*bake* / *heat* them in a pan and [4]*slice* / *season* with salt and pepper. [5]*Grill* / *Roast* some bread. Then [6]*fry* / *spread* the tomatoes on the bread and [7]*grate* / *season* some cheese on top. [8]*Fry* / *Bake* in the oven, but only for a few minutes – you don't want to [9]*overcook* / *slice* it!

3 Circle the verb which does not go with each food.

1 pepper:	chop	fry	spread
2 bread:	bake	roast	slice
3 chicken:	heat	overcook	grate
4 fish:	peel	grill	season

LEARN TO LEARN

Wordbuilding: adjectives from verbs

Learn the adjective form of new verbs. Sometimes the form is similar, for example *bake* (v) *baked* (adj).

4 Write the adjective form of the verbs in Exercise 1.

bake ______	overcook ______
chop ______	peel ______
fry ______	roast ______
grate ______	season ______
grill ______	slice ______
heat ______	spread ______

5 Which verbs in Exercise 1 usually go with the foods in the box?

apple bread cheese chicken chocolate egg jam meat tomato pepper

Grate … You can have grated apple, cheese, chocolate, egg, tomato and pepper.

Use it!

6 Discuss the questions.

1 Do you usually eat grilled, fried, baked or roast foods? Which are your favourites?
2 What can you cook?
3 Is it important to know how to cook? Why?

Explore it!

Guess the correct answer.

During the Chinese mid-autumn festival, people traditionally bake mooncakes. Which ingredient is baked inside them to symbolise the moon?

a chicken egg b ostrich egg c duck egg

Find another fact about a traditional food. Write a question for your partner.

Pronunciation p141

READING

An online forum

1 What types of food can you see in the photos? Which ones would you eat?

2 Read the forum and match comments 1–5 with photos A–E. (3.05)

1 ______ 3 ______ 5 ______

2 ______ 4 ______

3 Read the forum again and match the future food solutions 1–5 with the reasons a–e.

Future food solution	Why it solves the problem
1 Jellyfish	a cheap and already eaten in many parts of the world
2 Lab food	b can make new food from old
3 Smart fridges	c better for the environment
4 3-D printers	d help us use the food we already have so we don't buy food we don't need
5 Insects	e a new food and we need to find more of these

4 Match the words in **bold** in the forum with the meanings.

1 another possibility ______

2 the taste of something ______

3 not real ______

4 something special and good to eat ______

5 cooking instructions ______

A

B

C

D

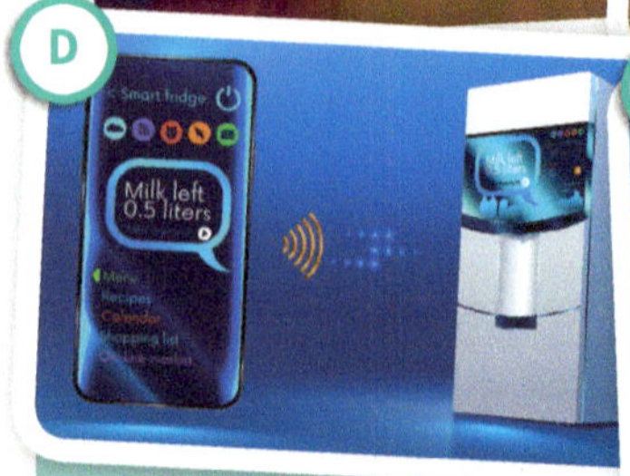

E

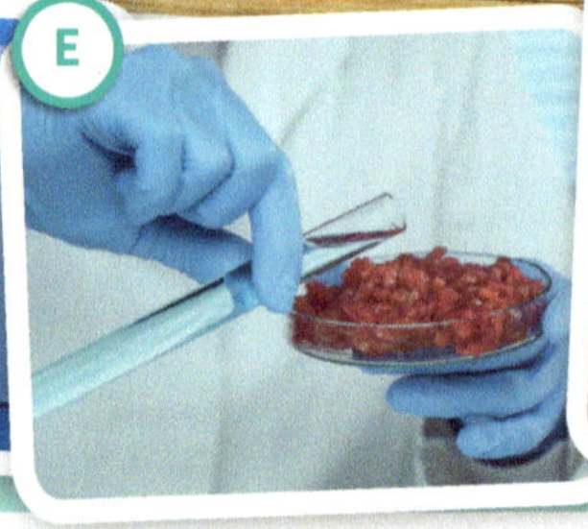

CLASS 4C STUDY ROOM

Read the article about future food and add your comments. Professor Jones is coming to Friday's class and we're going to discuss your ideas.

1 There isn't going to be enough food for everyone in the future because the population is growing, so we're going to need to be more adventurous and find new foods. I read that we could actually eat jellyfish, although many people won't like the idea. Jellyfish probably doesn't have much **flavour**, but if you season it and roast it, it might be quite tasty! *Abi*

2 We may eat **artificial** fish or meat grown in a laboratory in the future. I think the idea sounds disgusting, but scientists say it will be better for the planet. I'm definitely not going to eat lab burgers! *Ben*

3 We throw away far too much food, often because we buy more than we need. I read about these cool apps that will tell us what's in the fridge and suggest **recipes** with the food we already have so we don't waste so much. I think they'll be really popular. *Dana*

4 One thing I'm not sure about is 3-D printed food. The idea that a printer will produce our food is a bit strange. But people say we'll be able to print snacks from food we're going to throw away, so 3-D printers might help reduce food waste. *Marco*

5 Experts say that meat will be far more expensive in the future, so we're going to have to eat **alternative** types of food. Insects are cheaper than farm animals, so they may be a solution. Grilled grasshoppers are a popular snack in Mexico and fried tarantulas are a **delicacy** in Cambodia. In fact, lots of cultures eat bugs, so why can't we? *Emma*

Voice it!

5 Discuss the questions.

1 Which of the ideas in Exercise 3 are your most and least favourite. Why?

2 What other future food solutions can you think of?

Finished? p120 Ex 1

LANGUAGE IN ACTION

Future tenses

Watch video 3.2
What's happening this Saturday?
Which workshop might he go to?

Present tenses and *be going to* for future plans and intentions
Friday's class **starts** at nine o'clock.
Professor Jones [1]__________ **coming** to Friday's class.
We**'re** [2]__________ discuss your ideas on Friday.

1 **Complete the examples in the table above. Use the online forum on page 36 to help you.**

2 **Circle the correct words to complete the conversation.**

A [1]*Do you / Are you going to* watch the final tonight?

B Yeah. Kate [2]*comes / is coming* to my house to watch it.

A What time [3]*does it start / is it starting*?

B 8 pm, but she [4]*comes / is going to come* at 7 pm.

Get it right!

We often use the present continuous or *be going to* to talk about the future.

John's ***cooking*** *later.* **OR** *John's* ***going to cook*** *later.*

Predictions with *be going to*, *will* and *may/might*
The population is growing, so we [1]__________ need to find new foods. (a future prediction based on evidence)
We [2]__________ eat artificial fish or meat. (a future prediction we are not sure about)
Experts say that meat [3]__________ be far more expensive. (a prediction we are sure about)

3 **Complete the examples in the table above. Use the online forum on page 36 to help you.**

4 **Read the leaflet. Complete the dialogue with the present simple, present continuous, *be going to*, *will* or *may/might* form of the verbs in brackets.**

LUCAS Hey Milena, [1] are you coming (come) to Abi's birthday tomorrow?

MILENA Where [2]__________ you __________ (go)?

LUCAS To 'Dining in the Dark'. We [3]__________ (have) dinner in darkness!

MILENA That's strange. Abi [4]__________ (not like) it!

LUCAS I'm sure she [5]__________ (love) it! It [6]__________ (be) different to anything she's done before.

MILENA But you [7]__________ (not be able to) see the food. You [8]__________ (eat) something you don't like.

LUCAS I know! We [9]__________ (have to) guess what we're eating!

MILENA What time [10]__________ it __________ (start)?

LUCAS At eight o'clock.

MILENA I'm not sure. I [11]__________ (come). I [12]__________ (tell) you later.

Use it!

5 **Write the questions. Use future tenses. Ask and answer.**

1 What / you / do / tomorrow?

____

2 How old / you / be / in 2050?

____

3 What foods / we / eat / in the future?

____

4 When / your next class / start?

____

What are you going to do tomorrow?

I'm not sure. I might go to the beach.

Finished? p120 Ex 2

LISTENING AND VOCABULARY

Quantities

3.06 **1 Read the recipe and choose the correct photo 1–3. Listen and repeat.**

1

2

3

How to make your own fruity cereal

Mix the following ingredients in a bowl:

- a **cup** of cereal, like oats
- some **pieces** of strawberry
- some **slices** of banana
- some **chunks** of pineapple
- a **handful** of blueberries
- a **packet** of nuts
- a **pinch** of cinnamon
- a **sprinkle** of brown sugar

Serve with a **spoonful** of yoghurt or a **splash** of milk.

Nutritious and delicious!

2 Complete the sentences with quantities in Exercise 1 in the singular or plural form.

1 I have two _slices_ toast for breakfast and _____ coffee with _____ milk.
2 If your throat hurts, have _____ honey.
3 Season the pasta sauce with _____ salt and pepper.
4 I'm going to have a _____ crisps for lunch.
5 I love cookies with big _____ chocolate!
6 I make the best Greek salad. I put in _____ olives, some _____ feta cheese and _____ oregano on top.

LEARN TO LEARN

Using diagrams

Use diagrams to help remember new phrases.

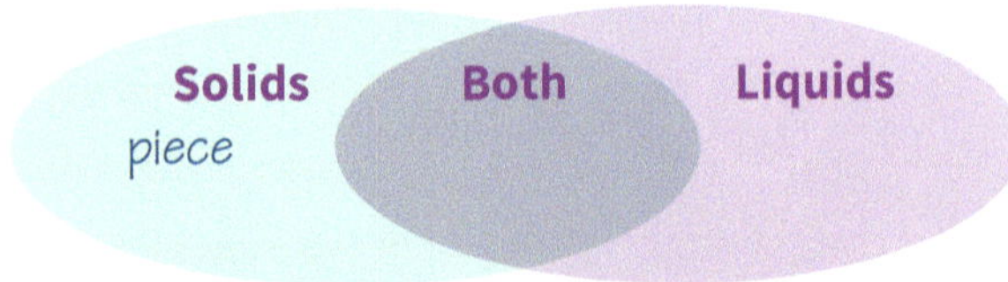

3 Add quantities in Exercise 1 to the diagram.

Use it!

4 Think of a food you like and tell your partner the ingredients.

A pancake … You need two cups of flour …

A recipe

3.07 **5 Listen to the cooking show and write the quantities.**

Pear smoothie	Ant tacos
1 _____ orange juice	6 _____ ant larvae
2 _____ chopped pear	7 _____ chopped tomatoes
3 _____ cricket flour	8 _____ chopped chillies
4 _____ mango and pineapple	9 _____ salt and pepper
5 _____ lime juice	10 _____ chopped coriander

3.07 **6 Listen again and circle the correct answers.**

1 Both of Anton's dishes ….
a contain insects b are spicy
c are Mexican
2 By 2030 there will be … billion people in the world.
a 5.5 b 6.5 c 8.5
3 Cricket flour will add … to the smoothie.
a fruit flavour b vitamins c protein
4 Anton is going to … the ant larvae.
a fry b heat c roast

LANGUAGE IN ACTION

Future continuous and future perfect

Watch video 3.3
Who will be making our food in the future?
What food was invented by accident?

Future continuous	Future perfect
I [1] ______ **making** a pear smoothie.	We [2] ______ **seen** and **tasted** some very unusual dishes
We [3] ______ **eating** a lot of meat in the future.	He [4] ______ **finished** by the end of the programme.
What [5] ______ you ______ **making**?	[6] ______ you ______ **finished** by the end of the programme?

Future continuous

1 **Complete the examples in the table above with *will/won't be* or *will/won't have*.**

2 **Complete the sentences with the future continuous form.**

eat not see stay ~~sleep~~

1 Don't ring me at 8.30. I *'ll be sleeping*.
2 Where ______ they ______ while they're on holiday?
3 I've got exams next week. I ______ my friends.
4 ______ we ______ insects in 30 years' time?

Future perfect

3 **Complete the sentences with the future perfect form.**

1 I think scientists *will have found* (find) life on other planets by 2060.
2 I ______ (not finish) my exams by the end of May.
3 They ______ (not start) yet. It's only 7.30.

3.08
4 **Complete the conversation with the future continuous or perfect form of the verbs. Listen and check.**

ZOE How [1] *will* restaurants *have changed* (change) by 2030?
SAM I think they [2] ______ (become) more automatic. Instead of human chefs, machines [3] ______ (cook) your food and human waiters [4] ______ (not serve) the tables, robots will.
ZOE So humans [5] ______ (not work) in restaurants?
SAM That's right, but I think we [6] ______ (design) robots that look like humans by then.

Use it!

5 **Write sentences about your future. Use the future continuous or perfect.**

In one years' time …
In 2050 …
On my 21st birthday …
By the end of this year …
By 2030 …
By the time I'm 25 …

In 2050 I'll be living in my own house.
By the time I'm 25 I'll have learned how to drive.

6 **Tell your partner your sentences about the future, but change some so that they are false. Can they guess which sentences are true and which are false?**

In 2050 I won't be living in my own house.

False?

Yes, it's false.

Finished? p120 Ex 3

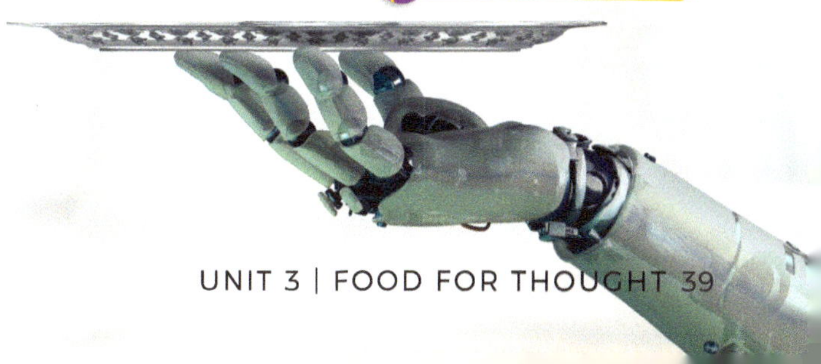

SPEAKING
Giving instructions

3.09 **1** **What can you see in the photo? What ingredients do you need to make it? Listen and check your answers.**

3.09 **2** **Complete the conversation with the phrases from the *Useful language* box. Listen and check.**

ROB Can you give me the recipe for your yummy Spanish omelette? I'm going to make it for the picnic tomorrow. It won't take ages, will it?

EVA No, it's a piece of cake! [1] _You'll need_ half a kilogramme of potatoes, five eggs, salt, oil and an onion.

ROB

EVA

ROB OK. Is that it?

EVA Yep, so [2] ______________ peeling and slicing the potatoes. [3] ______________, chop the onion.

ROB OK. Then what?

EVA Heat a cup of oil in a pan and fry the potatoes and onions.

ROB That's a fair amount of oil!

EVA Yeah, I know! [4] ______________ frying, mix the eggs in a bowl. Then put everything together and add a pinch of salt. Heat a spoonful of oil in a smaller pan and pour in the mixture. Once the bottom part has cooked, [5] ______________ flip the omelette with a plate and cook the other side.

ROB OK, I'll try.

EVA It's delicious! Your friends will all be asking for the recipe! Will you still be there at four?

ROB Yeah, but we'll have finished the omelette by then!

Useful language

Don't forget to … (+ verb)	While that's … (+ *-ing*)
Once that's done, …	You'll need …
Start by … (+ *-ing*)	

3 **Match the phrases in the conversation with the meanings. How do you say these phrases in your language?**

1 something that's easy ______________
2 delicious ______________
3 Is that everything? ______________
4 quite a lot ______________
5 a long time ______________

Watch video 3.4
Everyday English

a fair amount   ages   a piece of cake
Is that it?   yummy

PLAN

4 **Write about a recipe and the ingredients you need.**

____
____
____

SPEAK

5 **Practise explaining the recipe to your partner. Remember to use future tenses, vocabulary from this unit and phrases from the *Useful language* and *Everyday English* boxes.**

CHECK

6 **Work with another pair. Listen to their conversation and complete the notes.**

What was the recipe for? ______________
____

What ingredients do you need?
____
____

Would you like to eat this food?
____

WRITING

A listicle

1 What food can you see in the photos? Read Megan's listicle. Which of her predictions do you agree with?

2 The following are features of a good listicle. Which ones are in Megan's listicle?

1 an interesting title
2 a number in the title
3 short texts about the title, one for each number
4 some interesting predictions
5 photos

FIVE FOODS WE'LL ALL BE EATING IN 2070!

1 If there's one thing we'll still be eating in 50 years' time, it's pizza!

We've been eating pizza since the 19th century, so we're not going to stop now! In the future toppings will change for sure, but pizza isn't going anywhere!

2 Tasty meat alternatives

With more humans on the planet, we'll need alternative sources of protein such as insects. What could be tastier than a sprinkle of roast ants on your salad?

3 Classics that will never die out!

Some classic British dishes, like fish and chips, will be around forever, although the fish will probably come from fish farms instead of the sea.

4 Printed snacks

By 2070 we'll be printing most of our snacks with a 3-D printer. Impossible? Watch this space ...

5 Veggies and vegans

Vegetarian food is here to stay! In 2070 being veggie or vegan, and avoiding eggs, milk and cheese, will be the norm!

3 Read Megan's listicle again and make two lists.

Food that will be the same	Food that will be new
pizza	

4 Complete the *Useful language* phrases with the words in the box. Check in Megan's listicle.

anywhere forever norm space stay

Useful language

is here to [1] ______
isn't going [2] ______
Watch this [3] ______
will be around [4] ______
will be the [5] ______

Write your own listicle.

PLAN

5 Look at the questions and make notes.

1 What will people still be eating in 50 years' time?
2 What might we start eating in the future?
3 Which dishes will be around forever?
4 What food is unusual now but will be normal in the future?

WRITE

6 Write a listicle about your future food predictions. Remember to include future tenses, vocabulary from this unit and phrases from the *Useful language* box.

CHECK

7 Do you ...

- explain what we will or might be eating in the future?
- explain what will be normal in the future?
- make any other predictions?

Finished? p120 Ex 4

AROUND THE WORLD

READING
An article

3.10 **1** **Look at the photos. What can you see? What do they tell you about food in Australia? Read the article and check your ideas.**

Globetrotters

Watch video 3.5
Food in Japan

- What food is usually associated with your country or culture?
- Can you explain what *kaiseki* and *wagashi* are?
- How is Western food influencing Japanese food traditions?

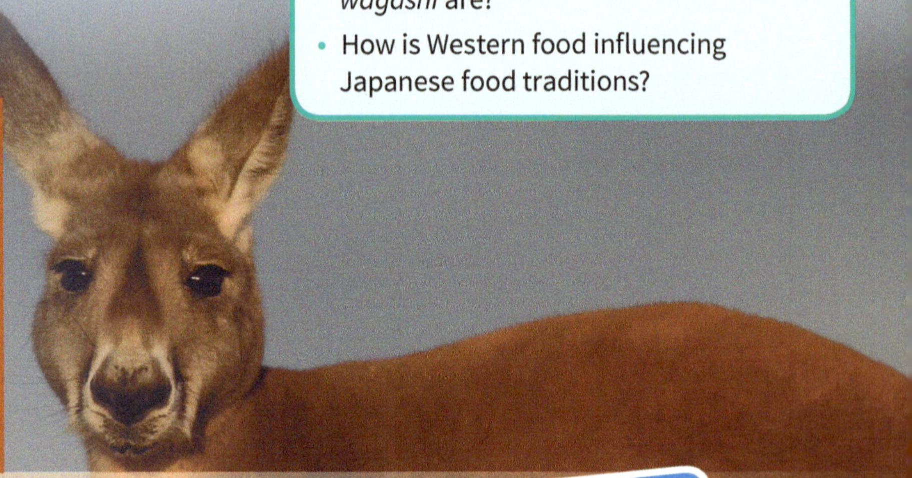

A TASTE OF *Australia*

A country's food is influenced by its inhabitants, geography, climate and wildlife, and Australia is no exception.

Traditional Australia

For thousands of years, the indigenous people of Australia have eaten plants and animals from the land or sea. Traditional Aboriginal food, or 'bush tucker', includes crocodile, emu and snake. Examples that are still eaten today include kangaroo, macadamia nuts and witchetty grubs. These tasty insect larvae are roasted on the fire or grilled on the barbecue!

Multicultural Australia

Since the first Europeans arrived in Australia over 200 years ago, people have been moving to the country from all over the world. As a result, Australian cuisine is multicultural and includes British, Italian, Greek and Asian food. Popular dishes are fish and chips, roast lamb and dim sum as well as traditional favourites such as kangaroo, seafood pizza and fried shark. The warm, sunny climate means plenty of fresh fruit and vegetables, and barbecues to grill meat or fish outside.

Tomorrow's Australia

Desert food

Australia has built the first farm in the world that can grow fruit and veg in a desert. The enormous solar-powered greenhouse only needs sunshine and seawater to work and Australia has plenty of both. The solar panels create enough energy to transform the salt water into fresh water which is used to water the tomato plants. It's strange to think that in the future we might be eating food which is grown in the desert.

Ugly food

Around a quarter of fruit and vegetables around the world is thrown away before it gets to the supermarkets because people believe it's too 'ugly' to sell. However, some Australian supermarkets are trying to sell this food. They tell their customers that even though the food looks odd, it tastes exactly the same as perfectly formed fruit and veg. There are lots of advantages to eating this ugly food. It's cheaper for customers, farmers sell more of their produce and we reduce food waste.

LEARN TO LEARN

Understanding words from context

When you see new words, use the rest of the sentence to help you understand them. Guess what the new word means and then check it in a dictionary.

2 **Find the words in the article and guess the meaning. Check in a dictionary or with your teacher.**

New word	What the other words tell me	What I think it means
1 indigenous	*It's an adjective that describes people who have lived in Australia for a long time.*	*original, first*
2 witchetty grubs		
3 multicultural		
4 shark		
5 solar-powered		
6 greenhouse		

3 **Read the article again and find examples of how these things influence Australia's food.**

Indigenous people

They have always eaten food from the land and sea and some is still eaten today, e.g. macadamia nuts and witchetty grubs.

Wildlife

______

______

People from other cultures

______

______

Climate

______

______

Food waste

______

______

4 **Find words in the article that mean:**

1 something not included in a group (introduction) ______
2 delicious (traditional Australia) ______
3 cooking (multicultural Australia) ______
4 a short word for vegetable (desert food) ______
5 strange (ugly food) ______

Voice it!

5 **Discuss the questions.**

1 Which foods from other cultures have become popular in your country?
2 Australia is adapting to changes by eating 'ugly' food. How else can we adapt what we eat or drink?

Explore it!

Guess the correct answer.

What will you not find on a pizza in Australia?

a emu b kangaroo c koala d crocodile

Find a fact about Australian food. Write a question for your partner to answer.

OWN IT! The Culture Project Teacher's Resource Bank

3 REVIEW

VOCABULARY

1 Circle the correct verbs.

1. *Season* / *Peel* the orange before you eat it.
2. Is there any butter to *spread* / *grate* on my toast?
3. Let's *roast* / *fry* a chicken in the oven.
4. Can I borrow a knife to *grill* / *slice* the tomato?
5. Sam *bakes* / *chops* his own bread. It's great!

2 Match the quantities with the photos. Then think of another example for each quantity.

chunk	☐	______	cup	☐	______
handful	☐	______	packet	☐	______
piece	☐	______	pinch	☐	______
slice	☐	______	splash	☐	______
spoonful	☐	______	sprinkle	☐	______

1

2

3

4

5

6

7

8

9

10

LANGUAGE IN ACTION

3 Circle the correct words to complete the conversation.

IVAN	What [1]*do you / are you going* to do this afternoon?
ANDREA	We [2]*'re going / will go* to the cinema. Juan and Ali [3]*come / are coming* too.
IVAN	What film [4]*are you going to / will you* see?
ANDREA	*The Scream Factor.*
IVAN	But you hate horror films!
ANDREA	I know! [5]*I'm not enjoying / I'm not going to enjoy* the film, but Ali wants to see it.
IVAN	It [6]*might be / is* OK. Who knows, you [7]*won't / may* enjoy it.
ANDREA	We'll see. Anyway, I have to go. It [8]*will start / starts* in 45 minutes.

4 Complete the predictions with the future continuous or perfect of the verbs in brackets. Which predictions do you agree / disagree with?

In 10 years' time …

1. African cuisine ________ (become) extremely popular.
2. most people ________ (stop) eating meat.
3. we ________ (not buy) 'ugly' fruit and veg.
4. we ________ (not go out) to restaurants. We ________ (order) food online to eat at home.

Self-assessment

I can use verbs to talk about food.

I can use words to talk about quantities.

I can use future tenses and *may/might*.

I can use the future continous and future perfect.

LEARN TO LEARN

LEARN TO ... SET AND ACHIEVE LEARNING GOALS

When you know what your English learning goals are, you can take steps to achieve them.

1 Read what Ada says about her learning goal. What is it? Has she achieved it yet?

In three weeks' time I'm going to New Zealand with my brother. He doesn't speak English so I'll need to book the hotels, order food and ask directions. My goal is to learn enough travel English to do this. I've bought a book with useful phrases for tourists, and I've downloaded episodes of a podcast about New Zealand. I'm going to listen to one episode every week. I'm also going to learn one useful phrase from the book every day. Piece of cake!

2 Write Ada's answers to questions 2–4.

Action plan		NAME: Ada
1	What do I want to do?	learn enough travel English to book hotels, order food and ask directions
2	How much time do I have?	
3	How am I going to do it?	a b
4	How often am I going to do the things in 3?	a b
5	What's my goal in one sentence?	By the time we go to New Zealand, I'll have learned enough travel English.

3 Read what Enzo says about his learning goal. Write his answers to questions 1 and 2.

One month from now we've got a speaking exam. I want to get a good grade, but I'm not great at speaking – not like my sister. She speaks English really well!

NAME: Enzo	
1	
2	
3	a b
4	a b
5	

4 Whose advice should Enzo take?

Why don't you practise with your sister? Ten minutes a day would help. – **Ela**

I'd study lots of vocabulary the night before. And don't sleep! – **Hamid**

Look at the Everyday English phrases in our book. Use three of them every day. – **Olga**

5 Use your answers in Exercise 4 to complete questions 3 and 4 of Enzo's action plan. Write one sentence about his goal for question 5.

OWN IT!

6 Think of an English learning goal. What are your answers to questions 1 to 5?

7 Tell your partner about your learning goal. Use the action plan to help you.

4 SENSE AND SENSITIVITY

LEARNING OUTCOMES

I can ...

- understand texts about people who don't feel pain or fear and artists who make sound effects
- make guesses and give clues about unfamiliar objects
- write an encyclopaedia entry
- make deductions and express obligation, prohibition, necessity and advice
- talk about senses and describe how things look, sound and feel, etc.
- brainstorm and use visual clues when listening
- create an infographic.

Start it!

1 Look at the photo. What different senses do you use when you enjoy an ice cream?
2 Before you watch, what do you think bats, dolphins and submarines have in common?
3 Which animal has the best hearing and how does that help them? Watch and check.
4 Can you think of any other animals which have special senses?

Watch video 4.1

p49

Language in action 4.2

p51

Language in action 4.3

p52

Everyday English 4.4

VOCABULARY
The five senses

1 **Match the words in bold with photos A–E. Answer the questions.**

Have you ever:

1 seen a **durian**? ☐
2 touched a **snake**? ☐
3 played football on **artificial grass**? ☐
4 heard a **koala**? ☐
5 eaten a **knickerbocker glory**? ☐

2 **Match the questions in Exercise 1 with statements a–e. Which things did you already know?**

a They **look like** friendly teddy bears but when they cry they **sound** really angry. 4
b It's made of plastic but it can often **feel like** the real thing. ☐
c It doesn't **sound like** a food but it is! They **taste** really sweet and look really colourful. ☐
d They **look** wet and slimy but when you **touch** their skin they **feel** cold and dry. ☐
e They **smell** terrible. In fact, they **smell like** dirty old socks and they don't **taste like** fruit, but many people say they're delicious. ☐

LEARN TO LEARN

Brainstorming

Brainstorming word groups can help you make vocabulary connections.

3 **Complete each line with the words in bold in Exercise 2. Add three or more words or phrases that you associate with them.**

a The ears: sound, sound like, hear, listen to, music
b The eyes: ____________
c The hands: ____________
d The nose: ____________
e The tongue: ____________

4 **Choose one group of words in Exercise 3. Say your extra words to your partner. Can they guess which group they belong to?**

5 **Complete the sentences with the correct form of the words in bold in Exercise 2.**

1 When my dad sleeps, he snores so much he sounds like a trumpet!
2 I tried some crocodile meat once. It ____________ chicken.
3 The milk ____________ bad and ____________ a bit yellow, so she didn't taste it.
4 I love wearing my new winter coat. It ____________ so soft and warm.
5 A It ____________ a painting by Picasso.
B No, but it is.
6 Please ____________ the wall. I've just painted it.

Use it!

6 **Talk about the things in the box with the words in Exercise 2. Compare with another pair. Do you have the same descriptions?**

fast food	graffiti	mobile phones	new clothes	rap music

Explore it!

Guess the correct answer.

Which human sense is the weakest?

a sight b hearing c touch
d taste e smell

Find another interesting fact about the human senses. Write a question for your partner to answer.

READING

A magazine article

1 Imagine you couldn't feel pain or fear. Would your life be better or worse? Why?

4.01 2 Read the magazine article. Which problems does it mention?

No pain, no fear – NO WAY!

Everybody knows what pain feels like. It's horrible. So imagine never feeling physical pain. You cut your finger – nothing. You break your leg – no pain at all. It must be wonderful, right? Wrong, because pain is the body's way of telling the brain that there's a problem. But some people, like Amy Campbell, can't feel pain. When she was born, Amy looked like an ordinary baby, but after a few months her parents realised something was wrong and thought she had developmental problems. She would chew her tongue and bite her fingers but she never cried. By the time she was a teenager, she had broken both arms and a leg – all without feeling a thing. It also doesn't matter if the air feels hot or cold, Amy can't feel the weather. But, like any young person, she has friends, hobbies (she plays the guitar), dreams and ambitions. She just has to be very careful. You may think her life can't be easy, but Amy is optimistic about her future. She says her condition affects what she can do, but not who she is inside.

Jordy Cernik

When Jordy Cernik tells people he feels no fear, they usually think he can't be serious. Having no fear might sound like a joke but it's not. During his 20s and 30s, Jordy had to have operations to remove his adrenal glands. Some time later, he realised that these operations had had a strange effect – he couldn't feel any fear. He did a parachute jump but didn't feel scared at all. He finds rollercoasters boring. Some people imagine it must be great not to feel fear, but there are disadvantages to not having any adrenaline. Adrenaline is a natural painkiller, so Jordy now feels more pain than ordinary people. It also means he doesn't feel excited about anything. Jordy now does 'scary' challenges to raise money for charity. Doctors think he could be the only person in the world who feels no fear, but knowledge about his condition may help them understand more common problems like anxiety.

3 Read the magazine article again. Write *T* (true), *F* (false) or *DS* (doesn't say).

1. Amy's parents knew there was a problem when she was born. F
2. Amy wears special clothes on cold days. ___
3. Amy doesn't think her condition affects her personality. ___
4. Jordy has never been able to feel fear. ___
5. Jordy loves rollercoasters. ___
6. There are probably many people like Jordy in the world. ___
7. Doctors think studying Jordy's condition could be useful. ___

4 Find words in the article that mean:

1. to break food into smaller pieces with your teeth. (Amy) ________
2. the things you want to achieve. (Amy) ________
3. a chemical produced by the body. (Jordy) ________
4. a chemical or drug that stops pain. (Jordy) ________
5. the feeling of being very worried. (Jordy) ________

Voice it!

5 Why do people enjoying doing scary things like riding on rollercoasters?

Finished? p121 Ex 1

LANGUAGE IN ACTION
Deduction and possibility

Watch video 4.2
Why is Andy an amazing athlete? How does he know when he's near the edge of the pool?

100% certain	It [1] ________ **be** wonderful.	
Possible	Having no fear [2] ________ **sound like** a joke. He [4] ________ **be** the only person in the world who feels no fear.	Knowledge about his condition [3] ________ **help** them understand.
100% impossible	He [5] ________ **be** serious.	

1 **Complete the examples in the table above. Use the magazine article on page 48 to help you.**

4.02 **2** **Circle the correct words. Listen and check.**

1 This drink (*must*) / *can't* have lots of sugar in it. It tastes really sweet.
2 Don't touch that snake! It *might* / *can't* be poisonous.
3 This milk *must* / *can't* be really old. It smells disgusting.
4 It looks like a painting by Monet, but it *may* / *can't* be. It was painted after he died.
5 A What instrument is that? It sounds like a violin.
  B Maybe, or it *can't* / *could* be a viola.
6 This jacket *must* / *can't* be very warm in winter. It feels like a blanket!

4.03 **3** **Complete the dialogue with *must*, *can't* or *might*. Listen and check.**

OMER What are you listening to? It's so loud!
BRIONY It's Beethoven. I think it's beautiful.
OMER You [1] must be joking! I thought you hated classical music.
BRIONY Well, that's because I hadn't really listened to any before. Did you know Beethoven became deaf when he was still quite young?
OMER Wow, that [2] ________ be easy for anyone, but it [3] ________ be absolutely terrible for a musician. You should turn it down, though. The neighbours [4] ________ be home.
BRIONY They [5] ________ be. The lights are off and their car's not there. Anyway, I'm sure they'd prefer Beethoven to the heavy metal you always play. They [6] ________ hate that! Every time you put it on they start banging on the wall.

4 **Write sentences about this situation with the verbs and phrases in the boxes. Use *must*, *can't*, *may*, *might* or *could*.**

Marco hasn't come to school yet. He has to give a presentation with his partner, Alice, and all their notes are in Marco's locker.

be	come	feel	have

a cold	in bed	late	nervous
soon	very relaxed	worried	

Marco might be in bed. Alice must feel worried.
____
____
____

Use it!

5 **Look at the photos. What do you think they are?**

It could/might/can't/must be ...

It looks like (a) ...

1
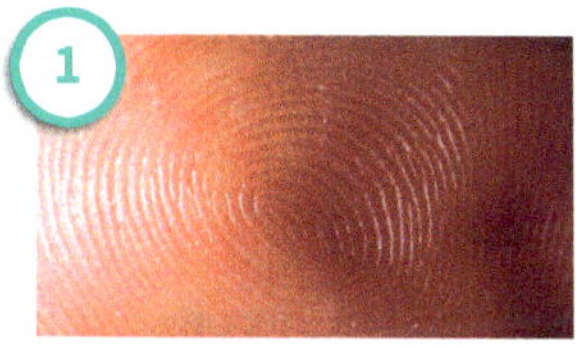

2
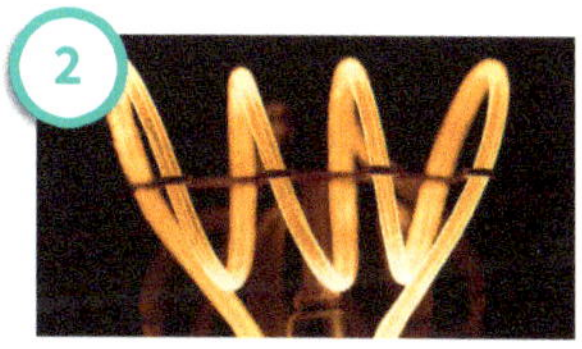

3

4

Finished? p121 Ex 2

VOCABULARY AND LISTENING

Describing texture, sound, taste, etc.

1 a sharp knife

2 a ________ umbrella

3 a ________ chameleon

4 ________ skin

5 a ________ chili

6 a ________ road

7 a ________ grapefruit

8 ________ balloons

9 a ________ skunk

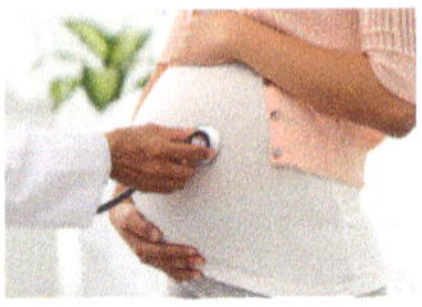

10 a ________ heartbeat

4.04 **1 Complete the photo labels with the words in the box. Listen, check and repeat.**

colourful faint rough ~~sharp~~ shiny
smelly smooth sour spicy transparent

2 Complete the table with the words in Exercise 1.

Feel	Look	Smell	Sound	Taste
rough				

Use it!

3 Use the words in Exercise 1 to describe the things in the box. Can your partner guess the item?

a cat's tongue a concrete wall a curry
a new coin a pencil a whisper lemons stars

It's shiny and gold.

A new coin!

An interview

4 Foley artists create sound effects for films. What sound effects do you think these items make?

a 

b 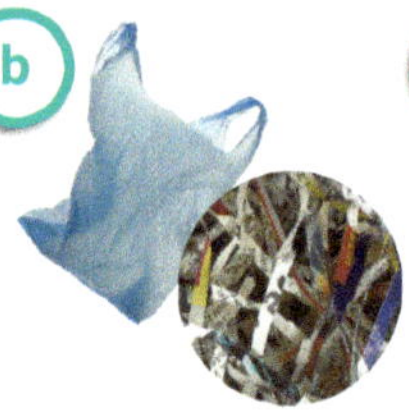

c 

d 

e 

a two coconut halves
b shredded newspaper and a plastic bag
c cellophane
d celery
e rice and a metal tray

I think the coconut halves could be the sound of …

4.05 **5 Listen to the interview with James Ford, a Foley artist. Check your answers to Exercise 4.**

4.05 **6 Listen again and circle the correct words.**

1 It's important to *never* / *sometimes* have total silence in a movie.
2 The interviewer thinks the second effect is made with *newspaper* / *grass*.
3 Foley artists used to make *more* / *fewer* sounds.
4 James *made some* / *didn't make any* of the explosion sounds in his last movie.
5 To become a Foley artist, formal training is *necessary* / *unnecessary*.

LEARN TO LEARN

Using visual clues when listening

Use pictures, instructions, etc., to help you understand what you are hearing.

Voice it!

7 Do you think the job of a Foley artist will disappear in the future? Why / Why not?

Watch video 4.3
What is she giving advice about?
What three things do you need to do?

LANGUAGE IN ACTION

Obligation, prohibition, necessity and advice

[1] ________ (present)	[2] ________ (present)	[3] ________	[4] ________
They **must** sound natural.	We **need to** experiment a lot.	You **mustn't** speak loudly in the library.	We **should** listen to another one.
These days we **don't have to** do everything.	You **don't need to** have any formal training.		You **shouldn't** do that.
Do you **have to** work hard?			You **ought to** be a creative person.

Pronunciation p141

1 **Complete the headings in the table above with *Obligation*, *Prohibition*, *Necessity* or *Advice*.**

2 **Circle the correct words.**

7 TIPS FOR LOOKING AFTER YOUR EYES

1. Most of us [1]*mustn't* / *need to* use computers every day but too much screen time can be bad for your eyes.
2. You [2]*ought to* / *shouldn't* spend more than about 20 minutes looking at a screen without taking a break.
3. You [3]*should* / *shouldn't* avoid using your phone in the dark. If you want to read, you [4]*ought to* / *have to* read a book.
4. Some people [5]*don't have to* / *mustn't* wear glasses, but if you do, you [6]*should* / *ought not to* clean the lenses.
5. Buy a good pair of sunglasses: everybody [7]*needs to* / *mustn't* protect their eyes from bright sunlight.
6. Don't forget about diet either. It [8]*ought to* / *mustn't* include lots of green vegetables and fatty fish.
7. Finally, everybody [9]*doesn't have to* / *should* have an eye test once a year.

Get it right!

We don't use *must* in the past, only *had to*.

Past obligation

In the past, Foley artists [1] ________ create all the effects.
I **didn't** [2] ________ make those sounds.
[3] ________ your parents ________ study English at school?

3 **Complete the table above with the correct form of *have to*.**

4 **Match 1–5 with a–e. Listen and check.** 4.08

1. She didn't have to study hard for the exam
2. I didn't have to wear a uniform at my last school
3. Billy didn't have to get up early this morning
4. Mia had to go to the dentist
5. I got all the answers wrong

a. because it's a holiday.
b. so I had to do the exercise again.
c. because she had toothache.
d. because she's really good at English.
e. but I do at the one I go to now.

5 **Complete the text with the correct form of *have to* or *should*.**

Do your parents have old photos? You [1]should ask them – they might be interesting. In the past, when you took a photo, the people [2] ________ stand still. They [3] ________ smile but they did. The photographer [4] ________ be careful because photos were expensive. Now, you [5] ________ worry because you can take lots on your phone. Some people think we [6] ________ take so many.

Use it!

6 **Make notes and compare with a partner.**

- something you had to do in the past
- something you ought to do soon

What did you have to do?

I had to visit the dentist last week!

Finished? p121 Ex 3

SPEAKING

Making guesses and giving clues

4.09 **1** **Look at the picture. What are *tabi*? Listen and find out.**

4.09 **2** **Complete the conversation with the phrases from the *Useful language* box. Listen and check.**

Useful language

Guess again.
Guess what it is / they are.
I guess they must be …
Perhaps it's something (+ *adjective*)
They're definitely some kind of …

Watch video 4.4
Everyday English

Bingo! I give up! I guess so.
nice and warm/hot, etc. Sure, why not?

AIDAN Hey, do you want to see something cool?
ZOE Sure, why not? Wow! What are those?
AIDAN They're called *tabi*. They're from Japan. [1] Guess what they are.
ZOE Well, they're [2] __________ of clothing. They look like gloves, but they can't be, can they?
AIDAN Nope. They're definitely not gloves.
ZOE They're in the shape of an 'L', so I guess [3] __________ socks.
AIDAN Bingo!
ZOE But why is the big toe separate from the other toes?
AIDAN I'm not telling you. Try and work it out yourself.
ZOE Hmm. Perhaps [4] __________ traditional. Maybe Japanese people wear rings on their big toes?
AIDAN No, that's not it. [5] __________ again.
ZOE No, I give up!
AIDAN It's so that they can wear them with sandals with straps. The strap goes between the big toe and the others.
ZOE Oh, that's a clever idea! They must be nice and warm to wear.
AIDAN I guess so. I haven't tried them on yet.

3 **Complete the dialogues with the phrases in the *Everyday English* box.**

1 A Shall we watch a movie? B __________
2 It's __________ today. Let's have a picnic!
3 A Is the answer 23? B __________
4 A Chinese must be hard to learn. B __________
5 A One more guess? B No – __________

PLAN

4 **Write about something from your country that might be new or strange to a foreigner, for example a food or an item of clothing. How would you describe it?**

____

____

SPEAK

5 **Practise describing something from your country to your partner. Remember to use modals, vocabulary from this unit and phrases from the *Useful language* and *Everyday English* boxes.**

CHECK

6 **Work with another pair. Listen to their conversation and complete the notes.**

What did you hear about? __________

____

How was it described? __________

____

WRITING

An encyclopaedia entry

1 **Look at the pictures. What is attached to the man's head? Read the encyclopaedia entry and find out.**

1 [ ] Neil Harbisson, 27 July 1984

2 [ ] Neil Harbisson is known as the world's first cyborg artist. He has been colour blind since birth and has a special antenna connected to his skull that lets him 'hear' colours as different vibrations in his head.

3 [ ] Neil was born in Belfast in 1984 and grew up in Barcelona. At the age of 16, he started to make black and white art. In 2004, scientists developed his special camera and attached it to his head. With the camera, Neil can 'hear' 360 colours, including some which are invisible to the human eye. In 2004, when he had to get a new passport, the UK passport office said no at first because he didn't look like a human. However, they finally accepted his application. He must be the only official cyborg in the world.

4 [ ] Neil now makes colourful art, including 'sound portraits' of famous people and geometric paintings. He has had exhibitions all around the world.

5 [ ] According to Neil, all human skin sounds orange.

2 **Match titles a–e with paragraphs 1–5.**

a Artwork
b Other information
c Introduction
d Name and date of birth
e Life

3 **Are the sentences *T* (true) or *F* (false)?**

1 Neil has always lived in the same place. ___
2 Neil doesn't always wear his antenna. ___
3 Neil can experience colours that ordinary humans can't see. ___
4 Neil couldn't get a new British passport. ___
5 People in many countries have seen Neil's art. ___

4 **Complete the sentences with the phrases from the *Useful language* box.**

1 Stefani Joanne Angelina Germanotta ______________ Lady Gaga.
2 She ______________ 28 March 1986 ______________ New York City.
3 ______________ four she began to learn to play the piano.
4 She makes energetic pop music, ______________ songs like *Bad Romance* and *Alejandro*.
5 ______________ Lady Gaga, you can teach yourself art.

Useful language

According to …	… is known as …
At the age of …	… was born on …
including …	and grew up in …

Write an encyclopaedia entry.

PLAN

5 **These artists all have a physical difference. Choose one and make notes about them.**

photographer Roesie Percy
chef Adam Cole
rapper Sean Forbes

name and date of birth
their life
their artwork

WRITE

6 **Write your encyclopaedia entry. Remember to include five paragraphs, modal verbs, vocabulary from this unit and phrases from the *Useful language* box.**

CHECK

7 **Do you …**

- include information about the person's life?
- include information about the person's artwork?

Finished? p121 Ex 4

THE SCIENCE PROJECT

An infographic on animal senses

1 Work in pairs. Can you answer the questions?

1 Which continents do elephants live in?
2 How do they know where they are going?
3 How strong is their trunk (their long nose)?
4 What do they use their ears for?

2 Read the infographic and check your answers to Exercise 1.

How to research

3 Which of these things should you do when you research? Tick the correct answers.

1 Decide the main information you want before doing research. ✓
2 Use questions in search engines, e.g. *How well can elephants see?* ☐
3 Read articles from start to finish. ☐
4 Read the contents list of articles or the titles of sections and then decide what you need to read. ☐
5 Make sure the information is fact and not opinion. ☐
6 Only check information on one site. ☐
7 Take notes as you read. ☐

Elephants anc

Elephants' eyes are on the side of their head and have three eyelids, one above the eye, one below, like humans, and an almost transparent one they use to keep dust, dirt and water out. However, their eyes aren't very strong. They normally use their trunks to know where they are going. In fact, the leader of a group of elephants is sometimes blind.

Elephants can hear extremely well because they have big ears. They can hear faint sounds, including the calls of elephants up to 1.5 km away. Their ears are about $^1/_6$ of the size of their bodies. They also use them to keep cool.

Elephants have to move their trunk around and smell the air all the time in order to find water, so they have an excellent sense of smell. They can detect water up to 12 km away.

Elephants use their rough trunks to explore the environment and care for their young. They also use it to fight. The trunk can lift objects that weigh up to 250 kg. They can also sense tiny vibrations in the ground with their feet. Scientists think this must be the reason why many survived the Asian Tsunami of 2004. They felt the vibrations of the earthquake and moved to higher ground.

their **amazing** senses

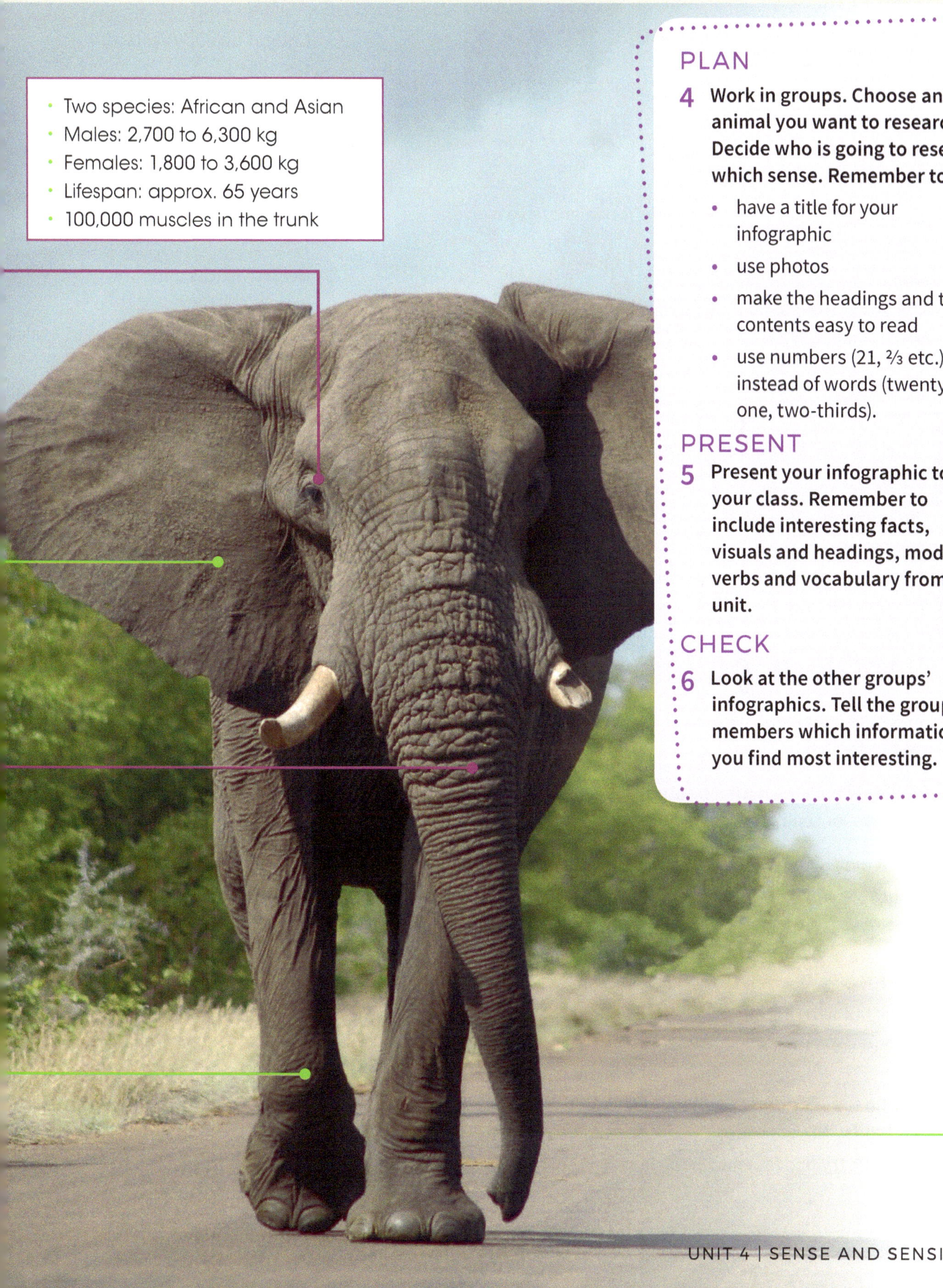

- Two species: African and Asian
- Males: 2,700 to 6,300 kg
- Females: 1,800 to 3,600 kg
- Lifespan: approx. 65 years
- 100,000 muscles in the trunk

PLAN

4 Work in groups. Choose an animal you want to research. Decide who is going to research which sense. Remember to:

- have a title for your infographic
- use photos
- make the headings and the contents easy to read
- use numbers (21, ⅔ etc.) instead of words (twenty-one, two-thirds).

PRESENT

5 Present your infographic to your class. Remember to include interesting facts, visuals and headings, modal verbs and vocabulary from this unit.

CHECK

6 Look at the other groups' infographics. Tell the group members which information you find most interesting.

4 REVIEW

VOCABULARY

1 Complete the sentences with the correct sense verb.

1 A Do you ________ your mum or your dad?
  B My mum – I've got the same eyes as her.
2 This coffee ________ incredibly sweet.
3 Your perfume ________ roses.
4 Your forehead ________ hot, Sam. You might have a fever.
5 Listen! Do you hear that noise? It ________ a mouse.
6 Ouch! I ________ a cactus!
7 I've just started to learn the guitar. I ________ very good yet, but one day I will.

2 Circle the correct words.

1 I don't like *spicy* / *smooth* food much – it burns my mouth.
2 I heard a very *transparent* / *faint* sound in the distance.
3 Are they new shoes? They're so *smelly* / *shiny* – I love them!
4 Be careful with that knife! It's really *sharp* / *faint*.
5 The pictures in that book are really *sour* / *colourful*.
6 These glasses are not completely *smelly* / *transparent*. You can't see the eyes of the person wearing them.

LANGUAGE IN ACTION

3 Complete the dialogue with *must*, *might* or *can't* and a phrase in the box.

be doing that	be right	be studying	be wrong	have football practice	know the answer

A What did you answer for question 10? I put 65.5.
B I put 75.3. We [1] ____________ both ____________. One of us [2] ____________.
A Shall we ask Tim? He [3] ____________. He's good at maths.
B Sure, but where is he?
A I'm not sure. He [4] ____________ in the library or he [5] ____________.
B No, he [6] ____________. Football practice is on Tuesday and today is Wednesday.
A OK, let's try and find him in the library then.

4 Match 1–5 with a–e. Complete the sentences with *have*/*has to*, *don't*/*doesn't have to*, *must*/*mustn't* or *had to*/*didn't have to*.

1 Eric got up early yesterday because he ________ ☐
2 This seat is reserved for old people so you ________ ☐
3 I've got lots to do tomorrow so I really ________ ☐
4 My friend had his car so we ________ ☐
5 Before visitors enter the exhibition, they ________ ☐

a sit there.
b start work at 7 am.
c take the bus.
d put their bags in a locker.
e go to bed soon.

Self-assessment

I can use verbs to talk about senses.

I can use adjectives to describe texture, sound, taste, etc.

I can use modals of deduction and possibility.

I can use modals of obligation, prohibition, necessity and advice.

LEARN TO ... PLAN YOUR HOMEWORK

When you have a lot of homework to do, it's important to decide what order to do it in and when to do it.

1 Ask and answer questions 1–4 in the leaflet with a partner. Are your answers similar or different?

Feeling stressed about homework?

With our useful advice, you don't need to panic!

How often have you ...

1 forgotten what you had to do for homework?
2 handed in a piece of homework late because you didn't start it until too late?
3 not started until you're too tired?
4 done the quick or easy homework first and then not had time for more difficult things?

If you answered 'often' or 'always', then you really need our help!

a Decide when you need to start your homework and give yourself enough time.
b When you ought to start but don't want to, tell yourself, 'I'll just do five minutes'. Once you start, it's easy to continue.
c You should think about how difficult a piece of homework is or how much time it needs.
d When you get your homework, write it down immediately and always in the same place.

Now use our homework planner and start planning!

2 Match advice a–d with the problems in questions 1–4.

1 ________ 2 ________ 3 ________ 4 ________

3 Helen is planning her homework. What should she do first and last on Saturday? Why?

Homework Planner **Student's name:** Helen

1 What is the subject and homework task?	2 When do I have to hand the homework in?	3 From 1–5, how easy/difficult is it? 1= very easy, 5= very difficult	4 How much time do I need to do it?	5 What day am I going to do it?	6 On each day, what am I going to do first, second etc.?
Maths, p38 Exercises 6–9	Monday	3	45 minutes	Saturday	
History, essay	Monday	5	1 1/2 hours	Saturday	
Science, p67 Exercises 3 and 4	Monday	4	1 hour	Saturday	
Geography, project	Wednesday	4	2 1/2 hours	Sunday	

OWN IT!

4 Think about the homework you have to do this week. Use the homework planner to plan it.

5 WONDERFUL WORLD

LEARNING OUTCOMES

I can …

- understand texts about smart cities and a virtual reality tour
- express surprise and disbelief
- write a competition entry
- understand how to use the passive, question tags and questions with prepositions
- use verbs related to processes and extreme adjectives
- learn verbs with prepositions, listen for specific information and skim read to understand the general idea.

Start it!

1 Look at the photo of the Northern Lights. What does it look like?
2 Before you watch, can you think of any natural wonders?
3 What does a waterfall in Yosemite National Park look like? Watch and check.
4 Which is your favourite natural wonder? Why?

Watch video 5.1

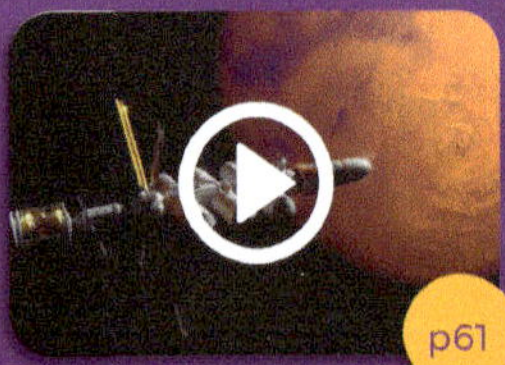

p61

Language in action 5.2

p63

Language in action 5.3

p64

Everyday English 5.4

p66

Globetrotters 5.5

VOCABULARY

Processes

5.01 **1 Read about three amazing animals. Listen and repeat the words in bold.**

2 Match the words in bold in the text with definitions a–l.

a make something exist *create*
b make something come nearer ______
c get a new quality/ability ______
d take somewhere ______
e find the size ______
f join ______
g bring together ______
h make something ______
i give ______
j find the answer ______
k share information ______
l use too much ______

LEARN TO LEARN

Learning verbs with prepositions

Learn verbs with the prepositions they take. This helps you to use them correctly.

3 Complete each sentence with a preposition (*to* or *with*). Sometimes both are possible.

1 Insects are **attracted** *to* spider webs.
2 Spiders **connect** their webs ______ something nearby.
3 Bees **communicate** ______ each other by dancing.
4 Bees collect nectar and **deliver** it ______ other bees.
5 Nectar **supplies** bees ______ nutrients.

Bees **measure** distances between new flowers and their hive. They **communicate** this information by dancing for other bees, which then **collect** the nectar and **deliver** it to the hive. Nectar and pollen **supply** the nutrients bees need to live.

Spiders **create** webs to **attract** as well as catch insects. The silk they **produce** is five times as strong as steel, but they have to wait for the wind to **connect** the end of the first line to something nearby. Spiders don't **waste** any silk: they sometimes eat their webs when they have finished with them.

Crows **solve** problems to get food. In some cities they **develop** the ability to read traffic lights; they wait for the red light, place a walnut in the road, then fly up and wait for a car to drive over the nut and break it open.

4 Circle the correct words.

1 Which puzzle has six sides and is difficult to *solve* / *deliver*?
2 Which North American country *measures* / *supplies* length in inches and feet, not centimetres and metres?
3 Which country *produces* / *attracts* the most films every year?
4 What's the name of the tunnel that *wastes* / *connects* the UK with France?
5 How do dolphins *communicate* / *develop* with each other?
6 Which animals *create* / *collect* nuts for the winter?

Use it!

5 Discuss the questions in Exercise 4.

Explore it!

Guess the correct answer.

Bees beat their wings very fast, but how many times per second?

a 100 b 200 c 300

Find an interesting fact about birds or insects. Write a question for your partner to answer.

READING

A webzine article

5.02 **1 Look at the photo. What do you think a smart city is? Read the webzine article and find out.**

2 Match headings a–d with paragraphs 1–4.

a Soon to become a reality
b Greener streets
c Everything will be connected
d More choices for citizens

3 Read the webzine article again and discuss the questions.

1 How will the IOT make urban life better?
2 What will 3-D printers be able to do?
3 How will food be delivered to our homes?
4 How will we be healthier?
5 Why won't electricity be wasted?
6 What percentage of people will be living in rural areas by 2050?

4 Find words in the webzine article that mean:

1 the number of people living in a place (paragraph 1) ____________
2 belong or relating to the city (paragraph 1)
3 a small flying machine without a pilot (paragraph 2) ____________
4 to stop something happening (paragraph 3) ____________
5 the people who live in a particular place (paragraph 4) ____________

Voice it!

5 Discuss the questions.

1 What disadvantages might there be to living in a smart city? Think of three ideas.
2 Would you like to live in a smart city? Tell your partner and explain your reasons.

Finished? p122 Ex 1

SMART CITIES OF THE FUTURE

1 ☐ Electric cars, drone deliveries, houses that communicate with you when you're out. Are you attracted by this image of city life? If so, you're not alone. Scientists and engineers around the world are developing a huge digital web called the Internet of Things (IOT) that will make all of this possible. Soon, billions of devices will be connected by the IOT. It will collect all sorts of data – information about the weather, the traffic, population movement, our shopping, the places we visit, even our health. This information will be used to make urban life better for everyone. Welcome to smart cities, the cities of the future.

2 ☐ In smart cities, we'll have more free time. For example, imagine you're feeling hungry on the way home but don't want to cook. All you'll need to do is send a message to your 3-D printer and tell it to print something tasty for you. Or, if you prefer, order a takeaway and within minutes a delicious pizza is delivered by a drone. Smart citizens will be healthier too. Our fridges will remind us when it's time to buy fresh fruit and vegetables, while devices on our bodies will measure our levels of fitness. The data they collect will be supplied to our doctors and we'll be told to visit them as soon as anything is wrong, so we won't be surprised by unexpected health problems.

3 ☐ Smart cities will also be better for the environment, because electricity won't be wasted in them. Imagine you forget to turn the lights off when you go out. Don't worry – your house will do it for you. What's more, streetlights will only be switched on when you walk past them and cars will communicate with traffic lights to prevent traffic jams, saving both time and energy.

4 ☐ When the first cities were built thousands of years ago, their inhabitants couldn't have realised how different urban life would become, but smart cities are nearly here. Will everything and everyone soon be connected by the IOT? Probably not, but by 2050 more than 70% of us will be living in a city, and we'll definitely be even more connected than we are today.

LANGUAGE IN ACTION
The passive

Watch video 5.2
How did people listen to music in the past? How will our clothes be made in the future?

Present	Past	Future
A pizza [1] ______ **delivered** by a drone.	The first cities [2] ______ **built** thousands of years ago.	Billions of devices [3] ______ **connected** by the IOT.
Time and energy **aren't wasted**.	Hieroglyphics **weren't understood** until 1822.	We [4] ______ **surprised** by unexpected health problems.
[5] ______ you **attracted** by this image of city life?	When **was** the Internet **invented**?	[6] ______ everything and everyone soon ______ **connected** by the IOT?

1 **Complete the examples in the table above. Use the webzine article on page 60 to help you.**

2 **Rewrite the sentences in the present or past with a passive form of the verb in bold and *by*.**

1. Moving objects **attract** bulls.
   Bulls are attracted by moving objects.
2. Lightning **strikes** men more often than women.
   ____
3. The Romans **didn't invent** Roman letters.
   ____
4. Elizabeth Magie **invented** Monopoly.
   ____

3 **Complete the text with the verbs in the box in the present and past passive.**

build	bury	lift	make
place	pull	use	~~visit~~

The Pyramids of Giza in Egypt [1] are visited by millions of tourists every year. When they [2] ______, about 5,500 years ago, great kings called pharaohs [3] ______ inside them. What we don't know is how the Pyramids [4] ______. More than two million blocks of stone [5] ______ for each one, but nobody knows how each stone [6] ______ in the correct position. Clearly, they [7] ______ by hand, because they were too heavy. [8] ______ they ______ by ropes or did people push them by hand?

5.03 **4** **Complete the conversation with the future passive of the verbs in brackets. Listen and check.**

A I was reading a blog that said in the future many jobs [1] will be done (do) by robots.
B Really? Like what?
A Well, food [2] ______ (serve) by them in restaurants, houses [3] ______ (build) by them – and in some schools, classes [4] ______ (teach) by them.
B Robot teachers! That will be strange. But [5] ______ all humans ______ (replace) by robots?
A I don't think so. The blog said most operations [6] ______ (not do) by robots – human doctors and surgeons will still do those.
B What about sports? [7] ______ human football players ______ (replace) completely?
A I don't think so, but who knows?
B I hope not, because that's what I want to be in the future!

Use it!

5 **Discuss the questions.**

1. Will all lessons be taught in English?
2. Will all shopping be done online?

Some lessons will be taught in English, but not all of them.

Finished? p122 Ex 2

LISTENING AND VOCABULARY

A virtual reality tour

1

2

3

1 Look at photos 1–3. Do you know where these places are?

5.04 2 Listen to the virtual tour and check your answers to Exercise 1.

LEARN TO LEARN

Listening for specific information

Knowing what kind of information we are listening for can help us to hear it.

3 **Read the sentences and decide if the missing information is a year, a measurement or a number.**

1 There are _seven_ New Wonders of the Natural World. _a number_

2 A major sports event took place in South Africa in ________. ________

3 The top of Table Mountain is ________ wide. ________

4 The biggest Komodo dragons are ________ long. ________

5 There are approximately ________ Komodo dragons on Komodo Island. ________

6 ________ smaller waterfalls make up Iguazu Falls. ________

7 The water falls up to ________. ________

5.04 4 **Listen again and complete the sentences in Exercise 3.**

Extreme adjectives

5.05 5 **Replace the underlined words in the text with the words in the box. Listen and check.**

boiling	deafening	dreadful	enormous	fascinating
freezing	gorgeous	marvellous	~~stunning~~	terrifying

The Sahara Desert looks [1]<u>very beautiful</u> _stunning_. I've been learning about it in class. It's [2]<u>very interesting</u> ________. At 9.2 million km², it's [3]<u>very big</u> ________. The sand dunes are [4]<u>very beautiful</u> ________. It would be [5]<u>very good</u> ________ to visit it one day, but it would be [6]<u>very scary</u> ________ to get lost there without water. During the day it's [7]<u>very hot</u> ________, but at night it can be [8]<u>very cold</u> ________. Sometimes there are sandstorms with [9]<u>very loud</u> ________ winds. It must be [10]<u>very bad</u> ________ to be caught in one.

Get it right!

We don't use *very* with extreme adjectives, but we can use *really* or *absolutely*.

Use it!

6 **Discuss the questions.**

1 Where can you find stunning scenery in your country?
2 Which is worse, boiling hot or freezing cold weather? Why?
3 Would you prefer to live in a gorgeous, tiny house or an ugly, enormous house? Why?
4 What's the most fascinating school subject? Why?

There is an enormous waterfall in my country. The noise is deafening when you stand next to it.

LANGUAGE IN ACTION

Question tags and questions with prepositions

Watch video 5.3
What is her vlog about?
What was she most impressed by?

	Positive sentence + negative tag	Negative sentence + positive tag
to be	It**'s** Cape Town, **isn't** it?	It **isn't** Sydney, [1] ______ it?
auxiliary *have*	The lesson **has** finished, [2] ______ it?	Ivan **hasn't** arrived yet, **has** he?
modal verbs	The speech **will** be recorded, **won't** it?	You **won't** be eaten, [3] ______ you?
present simple	You **speak** German, [4] ______ you?	They **don't live** here, **do** they?
past simple	Linda **went** home early, **didn't** she?	You **didn't tell** anyone our secret, [5] ______ you?

Question tags

1 **Complete the examples in the table above.**

2 **Complete the sentences with the correct question tag.**

1 That tour was very good, wasn't it?
2 Insects are interesting, ______ ?
3 It's not very hot in here, ______ ?
4 We can't hear each other, ______ ?
5 It would be scary to see a ghost, ______ ?

3 **Match the sentences in Exercise 1 with responses a–e. Complete the responses with the adjectives in the box.**

deafening fascinating freezing marvellous ~~terrifying~~

a Yes, it would be terrifying. [5]
b No, it's absolutely ______. [ ]
c No – the music is ______. [ ]
d It was ______. [ ]
e Yes, they're really ______. [ ]

Questions with prepositions

What are we learning [1] ______ today?	Where are we going [2] ______ next?
What are you looking [3] ______ ?	What are you scared [4] ______ ?
Who was it won [5] ______ ?	Who do you look [6] ______ ?

4 **Complete the examples in the table above with *about*, *at*, *by*, *like*, *of* or *to*.**

5 **Put the words in the correct order to make sentences. Then circle the correct answers.**

1 made / what / Tutankhamen's mask / of / was / ?
______
a glass b gold c silver

2 to / Apollo 11 / where / did / go / ?
______
a Mars b the moon c The International Space Station

3 a compass / what / for / used / is / ?
______
a making holes b drawing circles c cutting paper

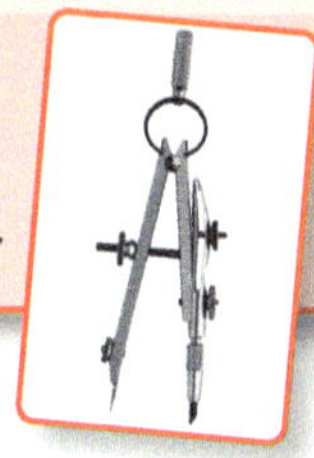

Use it!

6 **Discuss the questions using question tags.**

1 Who was *Don Quijote* written by?
2 What is a GPS used for?
3 What is glass made of?

Who was Don Quijote *written by?*

It was written by … , wasn't it?

Finished? p122 Ex 3

SPEAKING

Expressing surprise and disbelief

5.06 **1 What do you know about the building in the picture? Listen to the conversation. What do you learn about it?**

5.06 **2 Complete the conversation with the phrases from the *Useful language* box. Listen and check.**

ANGELA So, Ryan, how was your trip to Rome?
RYAN Oh, man, you should go. It's absolutely stunning. There's so much history and so many amazing buildings there. I loved it.
ANGELA Where was your favourite place?
RYAN I'd say it was the Coliseum.
ANGELA That's where the gladiators used to fight, isn't it?
RYAN Got it in one. Sometimes they would fight with animals, too. Bears, lions, elephants.
ANGELA You [1] can't be serious. With animals?
RYAN Yep. On one occasion over 10,000 animals were killed in a single day.
ANGELA [2] ______________ me? That's dreadful!
RYAN And they used to have sea battles there.
ANGELA I find [3] ______________. How was that done?
RYAN They would fill the stadium with water from the aqueducts. There were real ships and everything.
ANGELA: [4] ______________? That's fascinating.
RYAN Wanna see a photo of me dressed as a gladiator outside?
ANGELA OK, go on. Wow! Is that you? I can't [5] ______________ wore that!
RYAN I look terrifying, don't I?
ANGELA Er, not exactly. You look sweaty. It must've been really hot there.
RYAN It was. It was boiling.

Useful language

Are you kidding me?	Seriously?
I can't believe you actually …	You can't be serious.
I find that hard to believe.	

3 Complete the dialogues with the phrases in the *Everyday English* box.

1 A What's the best place you've ever been to?
  B ______________ Iceland.
2 A How was the movie?
  B ______________, I loved it!
3 A The exam was easy, wasn't it?
  B ______________. I think it was quite hard.
4 A Jack's house is enormous, isn't it?
  B I know! It's got a pool ______________.
5 A ______________ have a picnic tomorrow?
  B I can't, sorry. I'm busy.

Watch video 5.4
Everyday English

… and everything Er, not exactly.
I'd say it was … Oh, man Wanna … ?

PLAN

4 Write about an amazing place you have been to. Think of three interesting things about it.

SPEAK

5 Practise the conversation. Describe your amazing place and ask your partner about their place. Remember to use the passive, question tags, questions with prepositions and phrases from the *Useful language* and *Everyday English* boxes.

CHECK

6 Work with another pair. Listen to their conversation and complete the notes.

What place did they talk about? ______________

What was interesting about it? ______________

Would you like to visit it? ______________

WRITING
A competition entry

1 **Look at the photo. What do you think the building is? Read the competition entry and check your ideas.**

THE MOST INCREDIBLE PLACE I'VE EVER VISITED

1 ☐ I've been to lots of amazing places, but the one that impressed me the most was Petra, an ancient city in Jordan. I visited it last summer with my family. We all loved it.

2 ☐ Petra is fascinating. The first buildings were built over 2,000 years ago. At one time it was inhabited by 30,000 people. A lot of it was carved out of the rock of the mountains. In fact, it is sometimes known as 'the Rose City' because of the colour of the rock.

3 ☐ The highlight of a visit to Petra is the Treasury. Nobody is sure why it was built, but archaeologists think that a king was buried there or that it was a place for important documents. When the sun shines on the front of the building, it's really stunning. I'm absolutely certain that it will still be visited hundreds of years in the future.

4 ☐ I think Petra deserves to win because it is so beautiful, especially the Treasury. Without a doubt, it's one of the most incredible places in the world.

GO GLOBAL
Tell us about the most incredible place you've ever visited to win two air tickets!

2 **Read the entry again. Match topics a–d with paragraphs 1–4.**

- a The reason why the place should win
- b Introduction
- c Detailed description of part of the place
- d General description of the place

3 **Discuss the questions.**

1. What is unusual about the way Petra was built?
2. What do people think the Treasury was built for?
3. List all the extreme adjectives in the entry.

4 **Match phrases 1–5 with the phrases from the *Useful language* box a–e with a similar meaning.**

1. for me, the … that was best was … ☐
2. It's certain that … ☐
3. I'm completely sure that … ☐
4. … should win because … ☐
5. When you go to …, the best part is … ☐

Useful language

- a … deserves to win because …
- b I'm absolutely certain that …
- c The highlight of a visit to … is …
- d the … that impressed me the most was …
- e Without a doubt …

Write a competition entry.

PLAN

5 **Think of the most incredible place you have visited. Find out information about it and write down two reasons why it impressed you.**

WRITE

6 **Write your competition entry. Remember to include the four paragraphs in Exercise 2, extreme adjectives and phrases from the *Useful language* box.**

CHECK

7 **Do you …**

- give a description of the place?
- say why it impressed you?
- explain why you think the place should win?

Pronunciation p142

Finished? p122 Ex 4

AROUND THE WORLD

READING

A travel blog

Globetrotters

Watch video 5.5
Extreme homes

- What can make a place difficult to live in?
- Why is it difficult to live in these places: Atacama Desert, Siberia and Lake Titicaca?
- What's unusual about Matera?

1 **Look at the pictures. Where do you think they were taken?**

5.09 2 **Read Scott's blog for Day 1. Which activities that you can do in Meghalaya does he mention?**

____

____

____

LEARN TO LEARN

Skimming for gist

Often you want to understand the general idea of a text, not the details. To do this you can 'skim' the text, which means to read it very quickly.

3 **Skim the rest of the blog. Which of the activities that Scott mentions in Day 1 of his blog does he not do while he is in Meghalaya?**

____

Scott the Explorer

BLOGGING MY WAY AROUND INDIA

DAY 1

Hi, everyone! This week I'm in Meghalaya in northeast India, the wettest place on Earth. I've only been here for a day but I love the place already. It's really cloudy, but when the clouds lift the scenery is stunning: beautiful mountains covered by gorgeous green forests. The people are really friendly, and there are loads of things to do – you can go to festivals, explore caves, see waterfalls, visit a bird sanctuary, cross 'living root bridges', go trekking and so much more. I can't wait! This blog will be updated while I'm here so make sure you check out my posts!

DAY 2

This morning I went to the marvellous Siju Bird Sanctuary, where lots of endangered birds are protected. I even saw one of the rare peacock pheasants. Check out the photo! After that I tried *jadoh*, a local dish of rice and meat. Rice is traditionally eaten several times a day here, and it was delicious. In the afternoon I wanted to explore the capital, Shillong, where I'm staying, but it started raining heavily, so I stayed inside and relaxed. Tomorrow I'm going to visit the Krem Lymput cave. I'm really excited – I've never been in a cave before!

DAY 3

OK, I've just got back from the cave tour. It wasn't my favourite experience! The guide was great. He explained everything really clearly – how old the cave is, how it was made and so on, and the cave was beautiful, but at times I was really scared. It's over six km long, with some enormous rooms, but most of it was narrow, dark and wet. I had to carry a torch and walk really carefully. It was terrifying! Anyway, I'm safely back in the hostel now. More from me tomorrow!

DAY 4

Today I saw the Nongkrem dance festival. This colourful festival is celebrated by the Khasi people, who are one of the main groups of people in Meghalaya. They have an incredibly fascinating society. Women have a very important role in Meghalaya society. For example, the birth of a boy is not a special occasion but the birth of a girl is celebrated by everyone, children take their mother's surname, and when parents die, the youngest daughter gets their house. It's not the best place to be a boy. The sons don't really get anything!

DAY 5

DAY 6

I'm back! I didn't write anything yesterday because I was trekking in the mountains overnight. I saw some incredible views and finally crossed one of the famous tree root bridges. These bridges are created by hand. People tie the roots of young trees together and help them to grow slowly across rivers. The process takes many years, but eventually the roots are strong enough for people to walk on. Check out the picture I took! Anyway, the time here has gone so fast. I'd love to stay longer but tomorrow I have to leave. Thanks for reading!

5.10 **4 Now read the whole of Scott's blog. Discuss the questions.**

1. What problem did Scott have on Day 2?
2. Do you think Scott will visit any more caves in the future? Why / Why not?
3. What is unusual about births in Khasi society?
4. Why didn't Scott post anything on Day 5?
5. How are 'living root bridges' made?

5 Find adverbs in the travel blog that mean:

1. in a traditional way (day 2) ______
2. a lot (day 2) ______
3. in a way that is easy to understand (day 3) ______
4. absolutely (day 4) ______
5. in the end (day 6) ______

Voice it!

6 Discuss the questions.

1. Would you like to visit Meghalaya? Why / Why not?
2. Are boys and girls treated the same in your country?

Explore it!

Guess the correct answer.

Meghalaya is the wettest place on Earth, but where is the driest?

a in South America
b in Africa c in Australia

Find another interesting fact about an extreme place on Earth. Write a question for your partner to answer.

OWN IT! The Culture Project Teacher's Resource Bank

5 REVIEW

VOCABULARY

1 **Complete the sentences with the correct form of the verbs in the box.**

attract collect communicate connect
create deliver develop measure
produce solve supply waste

1 The postman ____________ seven letters to my house this morning.
2 The teacher ____________ the students' homework next Monday.
3 Scientists ____________ the Internet in the 1970s.
4 Most people ____________ lots of plastic every day.
5 My car engine ____________ a lot of heat.
6 Electric lights ____________ different insects.
7 Walt Disney ____________ some of the world's most famous cartoon characters.
8 A stopwatch ____________ time.
9 A young mathematician ____________ the most difficult equation in history a few years ago.
10 Three different companies ____________ electricity to this city next year.
11 The Channel Tunnel ____________ the United Kingdom with France.
12 Pilots on international flights use English ____________ with each other.

2 **Complete the sentences with the adjectives in the box.**

boiling deafening dreadful enormous
fascinating freezing terrifying

1 Turn that music down – it's ____________!
2 Can you open the window? It's ____________ in here.
3 It was a bad movie – the actors were ____________.
4 The Grand Canyon is 446 km long – it's ____________.
5 Put your coat on. It's ____________ today.
6 I'm scared of spiders. They're ____________.
7 The book was ____________. I read it twice!

LANGUAGE IN ACTION

3 **Rewrite sentences 1 to 5 in Exercise 1 as passive sentences.**

1 ____
____
2 ____
____
3 ____
____
4 ____
____
5 ____

4 **Complete the dialogue with the correct questions and question tags.**

A looking / you / what / for / are
[1] ____?
B My phone charger. It was here somewhere.
A You haven't put it in your bag,
[2] ____________?
B No, I looked there. You don't have an extra one, [3] ____________?
A Sorry, no. to / you / who / do / to / talk / need
[4] ____?
B My brother. We're going to a rugby match. It starts in 15 minutes.
A He can just wait for you inside the stadium,
[5] ____________?
B: No, because I've got the tickets!

Self-assessment

I can use verbs to talk about processes.	☹	😐	☺
I can use extreme adjectives.	☹	😐	☺
I can use the passive.	☹	😐	☺
I can use question tags and questions with prepositions.	☹	😐	☺

LEARN TO ... USE A PRESENTATION PLAN

A presentation plan can help you prepare a presentation and make it clear and easy for the listener to understand.

1 **Read Kirill's presentation plan notes. What do you think his presentation is about? Circle a, b or c.**

a a rainbow

b a total eclipse of the sun

c the aurora borealis

Presentation Plan

	Introduce the presentation.		Today, I'm going to talk about ...
1	*What is it?*		a very special event in the sky!
2	*How does it happen?*		the sun is hidden by the moon, parts of the Earth are covered by its shadow
3	*Where and when can you see it?*	**Where?**	You need to be in the area covered by the moon's shadow.
		When?	about once every year and a half
4	*What other information can I give you?*		Never look directly at it! It's dangerous.
5	*Have I ever seen one?*	**Where?**	Yes, in Russia
		When?	11 August, 2018
		What was it like?	absolutely stunning!

2 **Read the beginning of Kirill's presentation. Complete the missing questions.**

Good afternoon. Today, I'm going to talk about a total eclipse of the sun. Perhaps you've seen one. [1] What is it? *Well, it's a very special event in the sky.* [2] ______ *It happens when the sun is hidden by the moon and parts of the Earth are covered by its shadow.* [3] ______ *Well, you can only see it ...*

3 **Imagine you are doing Kirill's presentation together. Use the questions and the notes to do the complete presentation.**

OWN IT!

4 **Prepare a presentation on how a rainbow is formed. Use the information below to help you.**

How is a rainbow formed?

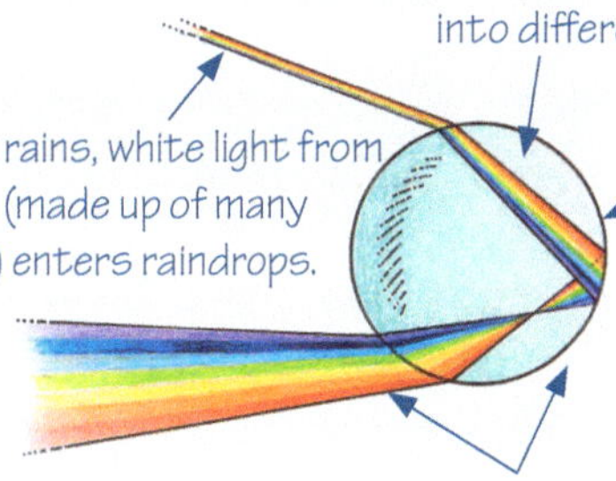

- We see the coloured light from all the millions of raindrops as a rainbow.
- You can see rainbows in the sky opposite the sun.
- Rainbows are really circles, but we only see half.
- If you're lucky, you might see a double rainbow

5 **Listen to your partner's presentation and ask a question.**

6 NO LIMITS

LEARNING OUTCOMES

I can ...

- understand texts about taking risks and overcoming challenges
- encourage a friend to do something
- write a for and against essay
- understand how to use conditional tenses
- use verb collocations with *get*, *take* and *have*, and talk about inspirations and challenges
- use collocations in sentences, and practise listen and choose questions
- make a leaflet.

Start it!

1 Look at the photo. Would you like to do a sport like this?

2 Before you watch, what extreme sports can you think of?

3 Why do people do extreme sports? Watch and check.

4 Are there any extreme sports you'd like to do? Which ones?

Watch video 6.1

p73

Language in action 6.2

p75

Language in action 6.3

p76

Everyday English 6.4

VOCABULARY

Verb collocations with *get*, *take* and *have*

6.01 **1** Read the quiz. Match the phrases in **bold** with definitions a–l. Listen and repeat the phrases.

a annoy somebody a lot *get on my nerves*
b become unhappy because something is not interesting ______
c do something that might be dangerous ______
d enjoy yourself ______
e be interested in something ______
f feel unsure about something ______
g get enjoyment from something ______
h have the possibility to do something ______
i not know where you are ______
j get a good feeling from something ______
k spend time with somebody so you learn more about them ______
l use the good things from a situation ______

1
A I **get bored** when I watch a film I've seen before.
B I **take pleasure in** watching films a second or third time.

2
A I like **taking advantage of** being in unknown places by myself to explore.
B I never walk around new places by myself in case I **get lost**.

3
A I **get a lot out of** extreme sports like skiing or waterskiing.
B I don't like to **take risks** and would never do extreme sports.

4
A I try new foods whenever I **have the chance**.
B I **have doubts** about trying new foods I've never eaten before.

5
A I like **getting to know** people who are exciting and unpredictable.
B People who are unpredictable sometimes **get on my nerves**.

6
A I **take an interest in** all kinds of fun activities, like going on theme park rides.
B I don't **have fun** on theme park rides. They scare me!

Did you choose more As or more Bs?
More As – You enjoy taking risks and like to experience new, exciting situations.
More Bs – You prefer not to take lots of risks and enjoy being in a routine.

Pronunciation p142

2 Read the quiz again. Circle the answers that are true for you.

3 Read the results at the bottom of the page. Do you agree with them?

LEARN TO LEARN

Using collocations in sentences

Collocations with *get*, *take* and *have* have lots of meanings. Record these collocations in a sentence to remember the meaning.

4 Think of true sentences for the collocations in Exercise 1. Use *always*, *usually*, *sometimes*, *hardly ever*, *never*.

I sometimes get bored when I'm at home.

5 Compare your sentences with your partner. What other collocations do you know with *get*, *have* and *take*?

Use it!

6 Write questions with the collocations. Ask and answer the questions.

______
______
______
______
______

Have you ever had the chance to try an extreme sport?

Yes, I had the chance to try waterskiing last summer. I had lots of fun!

Explore it!

Guess the correct answer.
How old was the oldest person to skydive?
a 89 b 102 c 110

Find another fact about an extreme sport. Write a question for your partner to answer.

When taking risks is a *good thing*

Everyone has to take risks sometimes, but many people think risks are negative, especially for teenagers. They connect risk-taking with dangerous behaviour, such as riding a motorbike too fast or looking at your phone while crossing the street. If this sounds like your parents, you might want to explain this to them. Taking risks can also be positive. Sometimes feeling scared or uncomfortable can help us experience new things and learn how to make good decisions. If more people understood this, they might see why teenagers sometimes need to take risks.

What type of risks do you like?

Surprises Would you be happy if your friends planned a surprise party for you? If the answer is yes, then you may enjoy unpredictable things. You get bored very easily and take pleasure in not knowing what's going to happen next.

Danger If you take an interest in activities such as skiing or parkour, you might enjoy danger. If you adore extreme sports or theme park rides, it's because risky situations produce a chemical in the brain called dopamine. Dopamine makes you feel happy and want to repeat an activity again to get the same feeling. That's why you want to go back on a rollercoaster ride as soon as it's finished.

New experiences Alternatively, if you have fun trying new foods or discovering new places, you may be someone who gets a lot out of new experiences. This is important because if you didn't go to new places, you wouldn't learn new things about other cultures.

Healthy risks

How would you feel if you had an audition for the school show? Auditions, selection to get into a school sports team or facing a school bully are situations that might make you feel scared. However, they also help you develop important skills such as how to solve problems, make good decisions and become independent. Just think, you could be the world's best singer, lawyer or volleyball player. But unless you take some risks, you'll never know.

READING

A fact sheet

1 6.04 **How do the people in the photos feel? How would you feel? Read the fact sheet and check your ideas.**

2 Read the fact sheet again and complete the table.

Types of risk taker	1 People who like unpredictable things. 2 People who like ______. 3 People who like ______.
Examples of negative risks	
Examples of positive risks	
Skills you develop when you take risks	

3 Read the fact sheet again. Write *T* (true), *F* (false) or *DS* (doesn't say).

1. All risks are dangerous. F
2. Most parents don't want teenagers to take risks. ___
3. Some people like not knowing what will happen. ___
4. You have more dopamine in your brain when you feel bored. ___
5. Taking risks can teach us about other cultures. ___
6. There are advantages to scary situations. ___
7. If you don't take risks, you won't solve problems. ___

4 Find words in the fact sheet that mean:

1. something that can change suddenly (adj) ______
2. love (v) ______
3. if something bad could happen (adj) ______
4. another possibility (adv) ______
5. choosing someone from a group of people (n) ______

Voice it!

5 Discuss the questions.

1. What type of risk taker is most similar to you? Why?
2. What risky things have you done that aren't dangerous, e.g. having an audition?
3. Can taking risks help solve problems?

Finished? p123 Ex 1

LANGUAGE IN ACTION

First and second conditional

Watch video 6.2
What did he try last week?
Did he like it?

First conditional	Second conditional
If this [1]________ (sound) like your parents, you **might want** to explain this to them.	If you **took** healthy risks, you **could become** more independent.
Unless you [2]________ (take) some risks, you**'ll** never **know**.	**If** you [3]________ (not go) to new places, you **wouldn't learn** new things about other cultures.
Will you **go** on all the rides **if** we **go** to the theme park?	**Would** you **be** happy if your friends [4]________ (plan) a surprise party for you?

1 **Complete the examples in the table above with the correct form of the verbs in brackets. Use the fact sheet on page 72 to help you.**

Get it right!

We can use ***unless*** to mean *except if*.
Use a positive verb with *unless*.
I'll go to the beach unless it rains =
I'll go to the beach except if it rains.

2 **Put the words in the correct order to make first conditional sentences.**

1 you'll / get better at it / If you / a lot, / practise parkour
If you practise parkour a lot, you'll get better at it.

2 from other cultures / if you / You might / try it / enjoy food
____

3 will you / doesn't rain / go to / If it / the water park / ?
____

3 **Complete the second conditional sentences with the correct form of the verbs.**

1 Would you learn to fly a plane if you had the chance? (would / have / learn)

2 If we ________ crazy things from time to time, life ________ boring. (could / be / not do)

3 I ________ frightened if I ________ in a forest at night. (wouldn't / get lost / be)

4 **Complete the text with the first or second conditional.**

If you [1]had (have) the chance, would you risk your life to save someone? If you thought about it carefully, you probably [2]________ (not put) yourself in danger, but scientists say it's a natural impulse. For example, if we [3]________ (see) someone in the water who couldn't swim, we would save them. In an emergency, unless we [4]________ (stop) and [5]________ (think) about it, the human body will react automatically.

Use it!

5 **Make questions with *you* in the first or second conditional. Ask and answer.**

1 If / not meet / friends / later / might / feel?
If you don't meet your friends later, how might you feel?

2 How / life / different / not have / social media?
____

3 What / do this weekend / have some free time?
____

4 Which extreme sport / try / could choose?
____

Finished? p123 Ex 2

VOCABULARY AND LISTENING

Inspiration and challenge

6.05 **1 Read the nomination for an amazing athlete. Match the words in bold with definitions a–j.**

Send us your nominations for the most amazing athlete you know and we'll tell their story on our podcast.

- Which athlete [1]**inspires** you because they have [2]**overcome** an [3]**obstacle**?
- Did they show [4]**determination** and [5]**bravery**? How?
- How did friends or family [6]**support** and [7]**encourage** them to get on with their life?
- What was their biggest [8]**challenge**?
- What have they [9]**achieved**?
- Have they had any [10]**opportunities** to help other people?

a deal with a difficult situation successfully ☐
b finish something or reach an aim after a lot of hard work ☐
c give confidence to others and motivate them to do something ☐
d give emotional or practical help to others ☐
e make someone feel they want to do something and can do it [1]
f no fear of dangerous or difficult things
g situations or chances ☐
h something which requires a lot of hard work to be done (successfully) ☐
i the ability to continue trying to do something difficult ☐
j something that stops an action or makes progress difficult or slow ☐

Use it!

2 Discuss the questions.

1 Who or what inspires you?
2 What's the biggest obstacle you or someone you know has overcome?
3 Who encourages you to do your homework?

A podcast

6.06 **3 Listen to the podcast. What big challenge did Bethany Hamilton overcome?**

LEARN TO LEARN

Listening and choosing the correct option

Read all the options, check any unknown words and cross out any options you know are not correct.

6.06 **4 Listen and circle the correct option.**

1 When she was 13 Bethany …
a learned to surf. b had an accident.
c gave up surfing.

- Check you understand *gave up* (past simple of *give up* – to stop something forever.)
- Option a isn't correct as she learned to surf when she was a young child.
- Option c isn't correct as she returned to surfing soon after the accident.
- The correct answer is option b.

6.07 **5 Listen to the whole extract and circle the correct options.**

2 Bethany lost her arm … .
a in the sea b in hospital
c three weeks after the accident

3 It was … decision to return to surfing.
a Bethany's b her family's c a bad

4 Bethany competes … .
a in special competitions
b only in the USA
c against other professional surfers

5 Her book and films … .
a are not true b teach people how to surf
c inspire people to overcome challenges

Voice it!

6 What surprises you most about her story? What would you do in a similar situation?

LANGUAGE IN ACTION
Third conditional

Watch video 6.3
What is she thinking about?
Where would she have gone on holiday?

[1]______ situation in the past	[2]______ consequence
If + **had** (**not**) + **past participle**	**would** (**not**) **have** + **past participle**
If they **hadn't taken** Bethany to hospital straight away, **If** that **had happened** to me,	she **would have died**. I **wouldn't have returned** to the water.
Question	
What **would** you **have done**	**if** it **had happened** to you?

1 Complete the headings with *Possible* or *Imaginary*.

2 Put the words in the correct order to make third conditional sentences.

1 had seen / she wouldn't / in the water / If Bethany / the shark / have gone

____

2 Many people wouldn't / if she / a film / have heard / hadn't made / about her bravery

____

6.08 3 Complete the third conditional sentences about stories 1–3. Use the verbs in brackets. Listen and check.

1 A girl got stuck under a car and a high school baseball team lifted the car off the girl.

a If the girl hadn't got stuck (not get stuck), the team wouldn't have needed (not need) to lift the car.

b If the team ______ (not lift) the car, the girl ______ (not survive)

2 A 14-year-old saw a fire in his neighbour's home and went to help and saved a boy.

a If he ______ (not see) the fire, he ______ (not go) to help.

b If he ______ (not go) to help, he ______ (not save) the boy.

3 A group of teens were attacked by a bear in Alaska. One girl did first aid for nine hours until help arrived.

a If they ______ (not go) to Alaska, they ______ (not be) attacked.

b If help ______ (arrive) earlier, the girl ______ (not do) first aid for nine hours.

4 Write a third conditional sentence for each situation.

1 Alfie broke his leg when he went rock climbing.

If Alfie hadn't gone rock climbing, he wouldn't have broken his leg.

2 Four students got up late and missed the coach to France.

____

____

3 The school cook didn't make enough food and the students were hungry.

____

____

4 Class 4B went to Madrid and learned how to speak Spanish.

____

____

Use it!

5 Complete the sentences about you.

1 If I had been born in a different country ______________________________ .

2 If I hadn't gone to this school ______________________________ .

3 If I hadn't met my best friend ______________________________ .

Finished? p123 Ex 3

SPEAKING

Encouraging a friend to do something

1 Listen to Mia and Jack's conversation. Which activities do they discuss? (6.09)

2 Complete the conversation with the phrases from the *Useful language* box. Listen and check. (6.09)

MIA Are you going to come whitewater rafting this weekend?
JACK I'm not sure. It looks a little scary to me.
MIA Oh, it's not really. I had so much fun when I went. [1] You'll never know unless you try, will you?
JACK But the water is so fast! It looks seriously deep and I'm not the world's best swimmer.
MIA Relax and [2] ________________. The instructors will look after you. They don't take any risks.
JACK Mmm, I'm still not sure.
MIA: Well what about paddle boarding? That's less risky.
JACK You've got to be joking! I wouldn't dare stand up on the board in the middle of the sea. [3] ________________ I fell in?
MIA Come on! It's easy! [4] ________________! If you fall in, you just get back on the board.
JACK [5] ________________, but I'm not like you. Water sports are a real challenge for me.
MIA Well, what if I practised with you?
JACK Hmm. That might help. OK, I'll come.
MIA Good for you! I promise [6] ________________ and you might even have fun! Let's go on Sunday.

Useful language

Encouraging
Don't worry, you'll be fine. You can do it!
You'll feel really proud afterwards.
You'll never know unless you try …

Responding
That's easy for you to say … What if … (+ past simple)?

Watch video 6.4 Everyday English

Come on! Good for you! not really
seriously You've got to be joking!

3 Match the phrases in the *Everyday English* box with their meanings 1–5.

1 extremely ________
2 not very ________
3 That's great! ________
4 to encourage someone to do something ________
5 You're not serious! ________

4 How do you say these phrases in your language?

PLAN

5 Make notes about something you want to encourage your partner to do. Use the ideas below or your own ideas.

do an audition for a school show
try an extreme sport

SPEAK

6 Practise trying to encourage your partner. Remember to use first, second and third conditionals, vocabulary from this unit and phrases from the *Useful language* and *Everyday English* boxes.

CHECK

7 Work with another pair. Listen to their conversation and complete the notes.

What did the other students encourage each other to do? ________________
Would you try the things in their conversation? ________________

WRITING

A for and against essay

1 Think about a time when something went wrong for you. How did you feel? What did you learn?

2 Read the for and against essay. Circle the best title.

a Is it always bad when things go wrong?

b Should we try more new things?

1 There are times when things go wrong. For example, you might lose a sports match or fail an important exam. However, is it always negative when this happens?

2 On the one hand, when things go wrong we feel bad. For instance, if we fail a French exam, we might have doubts about our ability to speak the language and lose confidence. Furthermore, we might think we haven't got the skills to achieve our goals.

3 On the other hand, when we overcome a difficult situation we feel good. If we think about what went wrong, we might solve the problem in the future, such as by preparing for our next exam in a different way.

4 In conclusion, although it can feel negative when things go wrong, I personally believe that this is not always bad if we can learn something new. When we look for an opportunity to overcome the problem, we'll soon feel good again.

3 Read the essay again and discuss the questions.

1 How does the writer end the introduction? Why?

2 In which paragraph does the writer give their opinion?

3 Which paragraph talks about the negatives?

4 Which paragraph talks about the positives?

4 Complete the *Useful language* box with the phrases from the essay.

Useful language

introducing a new idea: Furthermore …, [1] ________

introducing the opposite idea: [2] ________

giving an example: For example …, [3] ________, [4] ________

giving an opinion: [5] ________

introducing a conclusion: [6] ________

Write your own for and against essay.

PLAN

5 Look at the essay title and make notes on your ideas and examples. Decide what information to include in each paragraph. Use the information in Exercise 3 to help you.

Should we take risks?

WRITE

6 Write your for and against essay. Remember to include four paragraphs, conditional tenses, vocabulary from this unit and phrases from the *Useful language* box.

CHECK

7 Do you …

- include an introduction?
- talk about the negatives?
- talk about the positives?
- have a conclusion?

Finished? p123 Ex 4

THE CITIZENSHIP PROJECT

A leaflet

1 **Look at the leaflet. Which two things does it aim to do?**

a inform   b warn   c entertain   d persuade

6.10 **2** **Read the leaflet and answer the questions.**

1 Who are the courses for?
2 Which activities can you do on each course?
3 On which course will you work in a team?
4 The courses are 'unplugged'. What does that mean?
5 Why might it be good to try one of the courses?

3 **Read the leaflet again and find these features.**

1 Title
2 Introduction to get readers interested
3 Details about the activities
4 Phrases to persuade people to do the course

How to motivate yourself and your peers

4 **Match 1–4 with a–d to make tips about how to motivate yourself and your peers on a project.**

1 Be clear about what you have to do.	a All projects have problems. Find a way to solve them.
2 Don't give up when there's an obstacle.	b Divide up the work equally.
3 Each person has a role.	c Have confidence in yourself and your team.
4 Believe you can do the project.	d If you don't understand something, ask.

6.11 **5** **Listen to students working in a team at the start of their project. Put tips 1–4 in Exercise 4 in the order you hear them.**

___, ___, ___, ___

ON COURSE TO CONFIDENCE!

Are you 14–18? Do you get bored in the holidays? Do you like making friends, having fun and doing lots of exciting activities? If this sounds like you, then check out our courses and choose the one for you.

OUTDOOR SURVIVAL SKILLS

If you enjoy adventure and being outside in the fresh air, you will love this course. It's a great way to meet new people as you will be working in teams on different activities such as orienteering, building a fire and cooking outdoors. Some of the activities are challenging and you will have to work together and support each other to complete them.

WATER SPORTS

If your idea of fun is spending all day in the water, you will get a lot out of this course. You will have the chance to try everything from surfing and paddle boarding to scuba diving and whitewater rafting. If you've never tried water sports before, why not give them a go? You might be surprised at how much fun you have.

CLIMBING HIGH

One of our most popular courses is this confidence-building one. You will have the chance to go rock climbing and then abseil down again. You'll also go on a tree-top ropes course. If you'd like to learn a different skill, you could spend a day trying parkour.

Remember! All of our courses are unplugged, so leave your mobiles and other electronic devices at home. From day one you will discover that you don't have to be online to have fun.

We encourage you to take risks and try new things, so if you have never tried any of these sports, one of our courses is the perfect opportunity. Just think how good you'll feel if you overcome the fear to do something you've never done before!

PLAN

6 **Work in groups. Make a list of courses for teenagers to build their confidence. Then choose two or three ideas and design a leaflet to inform and persuade people to do them. Complete the steps below.**

- Draw a plan of the leaflet.
- Decide who prepares each section.
- Prepare your section with the features in Exercise 3.
- Show your section to someone else to check.
- Listen to your classmate's ideas and improve your section.
- Work together to make your leaflet.

PRESENT

7 **Present your leaflet to your classmates. Remember to include information about the courses, the features in Exercise 3 and the tips in *How to* motivate yourself and your peers.**

CHECK

8 **Read your classmates' leaflets. Decide which activities you would like to do from their leaflets.**

6 REVIEW

VOCABULARY

1 Circle the words which don't go with each verb.

1 get *a lot out of something / risks / lost*

2 take *pleasure in something / advantage of something / doubts*

3 have *on someone's nerves / the chance to do something / fun*

4 get *bored / to know someone / an interest in something*

2 Complete the sentences with the correct form of the words and phrases that don't go with the verbs in Exercise 1.

1 I had ____________ before I went rafting because I'm not a strong swimmer.

2 It can be positive to take ____________ because we learn to make decisions.

3 My brother has started to take ____________ photography.

4 My sister really gets ____________ . She's always taking my things.

3 Complete the sentences with the words in the box.

achieved	bravery	determination	opportunity	overcome	supported

1 She was awarded a prize for her ____________ in the fire.

2 My cousin finally ____________ his ambition to learn how to windsurf.

3 Do students have the ____________ to go to music classes at your school?

4 My parents ____________ my decision to do a bungee jump for charity.

5 He passed his final exams after a lot of hard work and ____________ .

6 Since I started swimming I have ____________ my fear of deep water.

LANGUAGE IN ACTION

4 Complete the sentences about parkour with the first or second conditional.

1 How quickly ____________ I ____________ (learn) if I practised every day?

2 If you already ____________ (do) regular sport or exercise, you may find it easy to learn.

3 If I ____________ (watch) parkour videos online, will I learn some techniques?

4 If you ____________ (train) every day for a month, you could learn to jump over walls.

5 Join the two sentences to make one sentence in the third conditional.

1 Mozart learned music as a young child. He wrote his first symphony when he was eight or nine.

____

____

2 Emma Watson studied drama as a child. She was Hermione in the Harry Potter films.

____

____

3 The artist van Gogh moved to Paris. Van Gogh met his friend Paul Gauguin in Paris.

____

____

4 J.R.R. Tolkien wrote *The Lord of the Rings*. Peter Jackson made a film trilogy of the book.

____

____

Self-assessment

I can use collocations with *get*, *take* and *have*.

I can use nouns and verbs for inspiration and challenge.

I can use the first and second conditional.

I can use the third conditional.

LEARN TO ... TAKE RESPONSIBILITY FOR YOUR LEARNING

It's important to take responsibility for your own learning. This will help you to learn when you are outside your class as well.

1 Do the quiz and find out your score. Do you agree with what it says about you? Discuss the results with a partner.

Are you taking responsibility for your learning?

	Always	Sometimes	Never
1 When you're in class, how often do you ...			
a pay attention to the teacher's corrections?			
b try to help your partner speak and write better?			
c use spidergrams and presentation plans?			
2 When you want to learn new vocabulary, how often do you ...			
a write example sentences?			
b make and use flashcards?			
c use a monolingual (only English) dictionary?			
3 Outside class, how often do you ...			
a speak in English to other people?			
b watch TV series or films in English?			
c read books or articles in English online?			
4 Thinking about technology, how often do you ...			
a have English as the language on your phone and your apps?			
b use vocabulary learning apps?			
c listen to podcasts in English?			
5 If you were travelling in an English-speaking country, would you ...			
a speak English in shops and restaurants?			
b try to understand signs in English?			
c ask for directions in English if you got lost?			

Extra challenges!

- Write text messages to your friends in English.
- Send and receive voice messages with friends in English.
- Listen to music in English and look up the lyrics online.
- Read a 'graded reader' – a famous book made easier for learners.

Points: always = 2, sometimes = 1, never = 0.

0–3 points: You aren't taking much responsibility for your learning yet, but if you try more ideas from the quiz, you'll soon become a better learner!

4–7 points: You're taking some responsibility for your learning, but there's a lot more you could do if you tried. Take advantage of what you've learned in this quiz to think about how to improve.

8–10 points: You're taking lots of responsibility for your learning. That's great! Time for something new – try our extra challenges!

2 Look at the extra challenges. Which is the best idea? Write one more.

OWN IT!

3 Think about how to take more responsibility for your learning. Choose three ideas and tell your partner what you have chosen and why.

I've chosen 'read a graded reader' because I love books. If I'd known about them before, I'd have started one already!

7 KEEP CALM!

LEARNING OUTCOMES

I can ...

- understand texts about a growth mindset and reducing exam stress
- express sympathy and concern
- write an email reply
- understand gerunds and infinitives, and subject and object questions
- use adjectives that describe feelings and expressions with *heart* and *mind*
- personalise vocabulary, make gapped flashcards, and learn synonyms and antonyms.

Start it!

1 Look at the photo. How is the girl feeling?

2 Before you watch, do you associate an emotion with these colours: red, grey, purple, yellow?

3 What colour can make you feel hungry? Watch and check.

4 What colours do you wear when you're happy and when you're sad?

Watch video 7.1

p85

Language in action 7.2

p87

Language in action 7.3

p88

Everyday English 7.4

p90

Globetrotters 7.5

VOCABULARY
Feelings

1 Read the leaflet. Do you agree with it?

7.01 2 Match the words in **bold** in the leaflet with definitions 1–13. Listen, check and repeat.

1 happy m
2 angry
3 unhappy
4 very silly
5 feeling thanks
6 not confident
7 enthusiastic
8 quiet and calm
9 in emotional pain
10 extremely happy
11 finding something funny
12 positive about the future
13 pleased to achieve something

7.02 3 Listen and complete the sentences with one word.

1 Sally feels absolutely ________.
2 The boy feels ________.
3 Mark felt absolutely ________.
4 The girl feels really ________.
5 Monica is feeling a bit ________.

LEARN TO LEARN
Remembering adjectives

Think about your personal experiences to help you remember new adjectives.

4 Do Part 1 in the Stay happy! leaflet. Think of a sentence for each adjective.

I feel amused when I watch comedy films.

5 Say your sentences. Do you have similar or different ideas?

I feel satisfied when I score a goal in football.

Use it!

6 Now do Part 2 of the leaflet. Tell your partner your plans.

STAY HAPPY!

For teenagers, life can be an emotional rollercoaster. Sometimes you're [a]**thrilled** to be alive, then you feel [b]**down** for no reason. You often feel [c]**insecure** about who you are, and [d]**annoyed** with every adult on the planet. You feel [e]**ridiculous** when you don't know something all your friends seem to know, and [f]**hurt** that nobody seems to care about what you're feeling. Of course, people do care, which is why we've created this exercise for developing positive emotions.

Part 1 For each word below (amused, etc.), think of a situation that helps you feel that emotion.

Part 2 Choose two positive emotions you want to practise. Do something which will increase those emotions every day for a week.

I feel …	This week I will …
[g]amused when my best friend tells me jokes.	ask him to tell me some every day.
[h]**hopeful** when I make a wish.	make three wishes about …
[i]**peaceful** when I walk on the beach.	
[j]**grateful** when people help me.	
[k]**eager** when I start a new art project.	
[l]**satisfied** when I've tidied my room.	
[m]**glad** when my friends are happy.	

Explore it!

Guess the correct answer.

Complete the expression *Laughter is the best …*

a communication. b exercise. c medicine.

Find out a fact about smiling. Write a question for your partner to answer.

READING

A magazine interview

1 **Read and answer the question at the beginning of the interview.**

7.03 **2** **Read the interview and match the interviewer's questions a–d with 1–4. Listen and check.**

a You had a fixed mindset?
b Malcolm, what exactly is a growth mindset?
c What advice would you give our readers?
d How can you develop a growth mindset?

3 **Read the interview again and circle the correct answers.**

1 Even if you have a fixed mindset, you …
  a never change.
  b are bad at maths.
  c can change.
  d like taking tests.
2 People with a growth mindset …
  a think they can get better.
  b are good at everything.
  c are scared of failing.
  d don't have to learn new skills.
3 Malcolm …
  a wanted to learn the piano.
  b played the piano for several years.
  c learned to play the guitar easily.
  d slowly improved his guitar playing.
4 Malcolm encourages readers to …
  a learn from their mistakes.
  b wait before trying new things.
  c ignore their mistakes.
  d try one thing at a time.

4 **Find words in the interview that mean:**

1 a feeling/opinion (question 1) ________
2 not changing (question 1) ________
3 without purpose (question 2) ________
4 necessary (question 4) ________
5 not a success (question 4) ________

The power of 'not yet'

Imagine you've just failed an important maths test. What do you think?

a I failed this test, but I can pass the next one if I study harder.
b I'm just not good at maths. There's no point trying.

If you chose a, you have a growth mindset. People with a growth mindset are often happier and more successful. But if you chose b, don't worry – you can change. I spoke to psychologist Malcolm Adams to find out how.

1 ☐ A mindset is your attitude to life. Some people have a fixed mindset. These people often avoid trying new things because they're afraid of making mistakes. They refuse to try harder, because they don't believe they can get better. On the other hand, people with a growth mindset believe they can improve with practice. They're eager to learn new skills and they're not afraid to fail sometimes. They often do well in life.

2 ☐ Let me tell you a story to explain this. When I was a kid my parents made me learn the piano. I didn't like the piano and it was really difficult. I remember feeling annoyed with myself whenever I made a mistake. After about a year, I stopped trying. I thought, 'This is pointless. I don't have any musical talent.'

3 ☐ Exactly. But later, at university, a friend said to me, 'If you want to be good at something, you have to believe you can do it.' So I thought, 'OK, let's try again.' I decided to learn the guitar, which I'd always adored. This time I told myself, 'You can do it!' I practised loads. It was hard, but little by little I got better. I'll never forget playing for my friends for the first time. I was thrilled! My mindset had completely changed.

4 ☐ Firstly, believe in yourself. Being positive is essential. Secondly, don't worry about making mistakes. A mistake isn't failure – it's an opportunity to learn. Finally, don't forget to use the power of 'not yet'. Never say, 'I can't do this.' Always remember to tell yourself, 'I can – just not yet.'

Voice it!

5 **Discuss the questions.**

1 Do you like to try new things? Why / Why not?
2 Where do you think you are on the scale for the activities in the box? Why? How can you change?

doing art	doing sports	playing music and singing	speaking English

1 ↑ fixed mindset
2
3 a mixture of both
4
5 ↓ growth mindset

Finished? p124 Ex 1

LANGUAGE IN ACTION
Gerunds and infinitives

Watch video 7.2
Why does Claire inspire him?
What did he try last summer?

Gerunds		Infinitives (with *to*)	
As the subject of the sentence	[1]Being positive is essential.	To explain purpose	[2]I spoke to Malcolm Adams to find out how.
After prepositions	[3]They're afraid of making mistakes.	After adjectives	[4]They're eager to learn new skills.
After certain verbs (*avoid*, *enjoy*, *finish*, *miss*, etc.)	[5]These people often avoid trying new things.	After certain verbs (*hope*, *refuse*, *would like*, etc.)	[6]They refuse to try harder.

1 **Underline the gerunds and infinitives (with *to*) in the examples in the table above.**

Get it right!

Some verbs, including *like*, *love* and *start*, can take the gerund or infinitive with no change in meaning.

*He **loves going/to go** for walks.*

2 **Complete the text with the gerund or infinitive form of the verbs in the box.**

develop feel help (x2)
increase ~~know~~ make say

THINK POSITIVE

You'll be glad [1] to know there are steps you can take [2] ________ a positive mindset. Psychologists suggest [3] ________ a list of activities that make you feel good, and then doing one every day [4] ________ your positivity. [5] ________ others when they have a problem also makes us feel happier. Of course, it's important [6] ________ thank you to people for [7] ________ you. Try it! Everyone wants [8] ________ more satisfied in life.

You can use the gerund or infinitive after *remember*, *forget* and *stop*, but this changes the meaning.

Gerunds	Infinitives (with *to*)
I **remember feeling** annoyed. *(= I have a memory of …)*	Always **remember to tell** yourself … *(= don't forget)*
I'll never **forget playing** for my friends for the first time. *(= I won't forget that memory)*	Don't **forget to use** the power of 'not yet'. *(= don't forget to do this in the future)*
I **stopped trying**. *(= I didn't do this anymore)*	I **stopped to rest** for a few minutes. *(= I stopped what I was doing for a while)*

3 **Complete the questions with the gerund or infinitive form of the verbs in brackets.**

1 Do you remember meeting (meet) your best friend?
2 When you're studying, how often do you stop ________ (take) a break?
3 What would happen if you forgot ________ (set) your alarm the night before an exam?
4 Would it be harder to stop ________ (use) your phone?
5 What things do you have to remember ________ (do) this weekend?
6 Think of two people you'll never forget ________ (meet) on your first day at school. Who are they?

Use it!

4 **Ask and answer the questions in Exercise 3.**

Finished? p124 Ex 2

VOCABULARY AND LISTENING

Expressions with *heart* and *mind*

7.04 **1** **Match the phrases in bold in the thought bubbles with definitions a–j. Listen, check and repeat.**

I have to [1]**learn by heart** so many facts for that exam but I don't have time!

What am I going to study at university? I have to [2]**make my mind up** soon.

I'm [3]**in two minds** about the party. I don't know many people there. Shall I go or just stay home?

[4]**I've got something on my mind** about school. Who should I talk to?

I want to become an actor, but what will Dad say? It'll [5]**break his heart** if I don't study science.

Education is a subject that's [6]**close to my heart**, but I don't know if I'd be a good teacher or not!

I need to choose my degree carefully. I can't [7]**change my mind** later.

I know if I [8]**put my heart into** this project, I'll do well, but I'm so tired!

It's just [9]**crossed my mind** that Dan might be at the party.

I must [10]**bear in mind** we can't use a pencil in the exam. I don't want to fail for something silly like that!

a consider something important 10
b make an effort to do something ☐
c think of something ☐
d make a decision ☐
e memorise ☐
f change a decision ☐
g unable to decide between two options ☐
h be worried about something ☐
i make someone really sad ☐
j be important to someone ☐

LEARN TO LEARN

Gapped flashcards

Flashcards can help you learn expressions.

2 **Make flashcards for some of the expressions in Exercise 1, leaving a gap for *heart* or *mind*(s). Write the missing word on the back. Then test your partner.**

be in two ______

minds

Use it!

3 **Choose six phrases in Exercise 1 and make sentences with the ideas in the box.**

clothes	friends and family	going out

When I go out in the evening, I have to bear in mind what time my parents want me to come home.

A conversation

4 **Which of these things do you think can reduce exam stress?**

1 studying late at night
2 studying with friends
3 drinking energy drinks
4 doing exercise
5 testing yourself
6 eating apples
7 making lists

7.05 **5** **Listen to the conversation. Circle the things in Exercise 4 that the counsellor recommends.**

7.05 **6** **Listen again and discuss the questions.**

1 Why is Gavin so stressed?
He's worried he's going to fail his exams.
2 Why does the counsellor suggest making a list?
3 Why does the counsellor recommend eating apples and nuts?
4 Why doesn't Gavin want to go to bed early?
5 Why is it important for Gavin to do well in every subject?
6 What is Gavin going to ask his sister tonight?
7 What was Gavin in two minds about earlier?

7 **Do you think the counsellor's suggestions are useful?**

LANGUAGE IN ACTION

Subject and object questions

Watch video 7.3
What's good about keeping a journal? Who helped her today?

Subject questions	
Who helps you?	My sister (helps me).
[1] _______ makes you think that?	Everything (makes me think that)!
Object questions	
Who do you want to teach?	(I want to teach) primary school kids.
[2] _______ she study?	(She studied) physics.

1 **Complete the examples in the table above.**

2 **Circle the correct words to complete the rules.**

1 The words in red are *subjects* / *objects*. The ones in green are *subjects* / *objects*.
2 *Subject* / *Object* questions always use a form of *do*.

3 **Complete the present simple questions with subject or object question forms.**

1 What do you do (do/you) at the weekend?
2 Who _______ (teach) you maths?
3 Who _______ (send) you the most messages every day?
4 Which subjects _______ (put/you) your heart into?
5 Who _______ (help) you with your homework?
6 What _______ (happen) if you don't sleep enough?

4 **Complete the past simple questions with subject or object question forms.**

1 Who taught (teach) you English last year?
2 What _______ (eat / you) for breakfast?
3 Who _______ (give) you presents for your birthday?
4 What presents _______ (give / they) you?
5 Which TV shows _______ (watch / you) yesterday?
6 Which country _______ (win) the last football World Cup?

5 **Ask and answer the questions in Exercises 2 and 3.**

6 7.06 **Complete the dialogue with the correct subject or object question form. Listen and check.**

OLAF What's that?
ROSA It's a stress ball.
OLAF What [1] does it do (do/it)?
ROSA It helps you relax. Look, you squeeze it like this. It was a birthday present.
OLAF Wow, that feels great! Who [2] _______ (give) it to you?
ROSA My sister. She knows I get stressed out a lot so she thought it might help.
OLAF I want one.
ROSA You don't need one! You never get stressed.
OLAF That's not true. Who [3] _______ (tell) you that? I get stressed before exams.
ROSA Well, you could borrow this one if you like.
OLAF No, I'd prefer my own, thanks. Where [4] _______ (get/ your sister) it?
ROSA Online, I think.
OLAF What site [5] _______ (use/she)? Do you know?
ROSA I'll ask her, but I'm sure you can get them in lots of places. They've been around for years.
OLAF Really? Who [6] _______ (invent) them?
ROSA No idea. Let's look it up!

Use it!

7 **Ask and answer the questions.**

1 Who did you call/visit/help yesterday?
2 Who called/visited/helped you yesterday?

Pronunciation p142

Finished? p124 Ex 3

SPEAKING

Expressing sympathy and concern

1 What problems do brothers and sisters usually have?

7.10 2 Listen to the conversation. What is Jerry's problem?

PAULA Hey, Jerry. What's [1]the matter? You look really down.
JERRY I am. It's my brother. He's refusing to talk to me.
PAULA Really? That's not [2]________. Why?
JERRY His tablet has stopped working. He thinks I took it without asking and broke it, but I didn't, I swear. Now when I try to talk to him he just walks away.
PAULA That's a little harsh, isn't it?
JERRY The thing is, he ought to know I wouldn't take his stuff without permission. I feel really hurt.
PAULA I [3]________. It's horrible when someone doesn't believe you. But bear in mind he's doing his final exams at the moment. He's probably really stressed out about everything.
JERRY I guess you're right, but I hope he calms down soon.
PAULA Is there [4]________? I have an old tablet I could lend him.
JERRY That's kind of you, but you don't need to do that.
PAULA Don't mention it, but let me know if you change your mind. It'll [5]________.

7.10 3 Complete the conversation with the phrases from the *Useful language* box. Listen and check.

Useful language

I can imagine.
Is there anything I can do to help?
It'll all be OK, you'll see.
That's not very nice.
What's the matter?

4 Replace the phrases in **bold** with the *Everyday English* phrases in the box.

1 Do I need help? No, **that's a nice thing to offer**, but I'm fine. ________
2 **I'm absolutely certain** my keys are here. I had them a few minutes ago. ________
3 Your teacher told you off for being two minutes late? That's **not fair**. ________
4 Of course you're **totally nervous and worried**. It's your final exams! ________
5 A Thanks for letting me use your desk.
B **No problem at all.** ________

Watch video 7.4
Everyday English

a little harsh   Don't mention it.   I swear
stressed out   That's kind of you …

PLAN

5 Make notes about one of the problems you thought of in Exercise 1.

____
____
____

SPEAK

6 Practise talking about the problem with your partner. Remember to use gerunds or infinitives, vocabulary from this unit and phrases from the *Useful language* and *Everyday English* boxes

CHECK

7 Work with another pair. Listen to their conversation and complete the notes.

What problem did they talk about? ________
____

How sympathetic did the conversation sound?
____

WRITING

An email reply

1 Look at the photo of a teenager and her mum. What do you think is the problem?

2 Read the email to a teenage magazine and the reply. Who is asking for advice? Who is giving it?

Dear Abby,

I want to follow my daughter on social media because I'm worried about who she might become friends with, but she says I can't because it would be 'totally embarrassing' if I posted on her wall. I feel hurt by her reaction. You're a teenager – how can I change her mind?

Many thanks,

Janelle

Dear Janelle,

I'm glad you wrote. Firstly, this is a common problem, so don't feel down. However, your daughter's reaction isn't unusual. It doesn't mean she doesn't love you, but she needs space.

I would recommend telling her why you are worried. It would definitely help to talk. Why don't you suggest following her, but promise not to post on her wall? If she isn't happy with that, it might be better not to follow her at all. Whatever you do, don't get annoyed with her and don't forget to tell her that you trust her.

Good luck, and let me know how it goes.

Abby

3 How useful is Abby's advice?

4 Look at the *Useful language* box. Find and underline the phrases in Abby's email.

5 Complete the mini-dialogues with the phrases from the *Useful language* box.

1 A So the party starts at seven, does it?
B Yes, but ________________, don't tell Pablo. It's a surprise.

2 A My best friend is stressed about her exams.
B ________________ joining a study group?

3 A Joe has to take his medicine.
B Yes, but ________________ not to wake him. He needs to rest as well.

4 A What's a good way to get fit and have fun?
B ________________ joining a football team.

5 A Felix isn't talking to me.
B Well, ________________ say sorry.

Useful language

It might be better (not) to …
It would definitely help to …
I would recommend … (+ *-ing*)
Whatever you do, don't …
Why don't you suggest … (+ *-ing*)?

Write an email reply to a worried parent.

PLAN

6 Imagine you are Abby. Choose one of the problems below to reply to. Think of three pieces of advice that they should or shouldn't do.

My son never does his homework on time. His teachers are angry and I don't know what to do.

My daughter refuses to help with the housework. She says she's too busy studying.

WRITE

7 Write your email reply. Remember to include the plan in Exercise 6, language from this unit and phrases from the *Useful language* box.

CHECK

8 Do you …

- say what the person should do?
- say what the person should not do?
- think the advice is useful?

Finished? p124 Ex 4

AROUND THE WORLD

READING

A report about schools in Denmark

Globetrotters

Watch video 7.5 Happiness around the world

- What different things can make us happy?
- Are Costa Rica and Norway considered happy countries? Why?
- What do Ecuador and Bhutan have in common?

1 What do you think is most important in making a school a happy place? Why?

a lots of events
b a nice building
c student clubs and sports teams
d technology in the classroom

7.11 **2 Read the report and put the paragraph titles in the correct place 1–5. Listen and check your answers.**

a Enjoying *hygge* is for everyone
b Conclusion
c Introduction
d Understanding other people
e Learning with others builds a better society

The happiest children in the world: a report

1 ☐

We have written this report to describe some of the reasons why Danish children are the happiest in the world. It is part of our school project 'Happier students, happier societies'.

2 ☐

One of the most important reasons Danish children are so happy is that they are taught empathy from a very young age. Empathy is the ability to imagine what it must be like to be another person. At preschool, Danish children learn to do this by studying facial expressions. They are shown pictures of the faces of other children showing anger, fear, sadness, etc. The preschool children say what they think the children in the pictures are feeling, and try to imagine being them. Schoolchildren never stop learning about empathy. Even 15- and 16-year-olds continue to have one hour a week of empathy as a compulsory subject.

3 ☐

Danish teenagers also have 'Class time'. This is a special time when students come together to talk about any individual or group problems they are having. This could be a personal issue between two students, or even something unrelated to school. During this time, everyone bears in mind the feelings of others and avoids criticising anyone. The group tries to find a solution together. They do this in a peaceful environment, with everyone glad to take part. 'Class time' is connected to *hygge*, a Danish word that is tricky to translate into English but which means relaxed and cosy.

4 ☐

In Danish schools students with different strengths and weaknesses study together in mixed groups. This helps to develop their empathy by showing them that everyone has strong points, talents and positive qualities. One student might find English difficult, for example, but be good at maths. Another might find English easy but find it difficult to understand maths. In a Danish school, these two students would help each other during lessons, and often between lessons as well. The system develops teamwork, respect and collaboration. These are essential qualities for a successful, happy life both at school and in the adult world.

5 ☐

In summary, the main reason that Danish children are so happy is very simple: they develop empathy, and empathy increases happiness by making everyone feel included and understood. They do this in a number of different but connected ways: learning to read the feelings of others, discussing problems together, and working in mixed groups. We believe that introducing any one of these methods into our own school would be straightforward and would improve our school life a great deal. Imagine what we could achieve if we tried all three!

3 Read the report again and circle the correct answers.

1 This report was written by …
 a teachers.
 b students.

2 Preschool Danish children look at pictures of …
 a their classmates.
 b children they don't know.

3 Danish teenagers …
 a can study empathy if they want to.
 b have to study empathy.

4 In 'Class time' students talk about …
 a all kinds of problems.
 b their individual problems.

5 In Danish schools, students with different abilities …
 a help each other in class.
 b help each other in and out of class.

6 To improve their own school, the writers suggest …
 a trying all the ideas in the report.
 b trying only one of the ideas.

LEARN TO LEARN

Synonyms and antonyms

Learning words with similar or opposite meanings can help you to increase your vocabulary quickly.

4 Complete the table with words from the report.

	Word(s) with a similar meaning	Word with the opposite meaning
joy	happiness	[1] sadness
[2]	obligatory	optional
[3]	single	[4]
related	[5]	[6]
difficult	[7]	easy
[8]	strong points	weaknesses
important	[9]	unimportant
simple	[10]	complicated

Voice it!

5 Discuss the questions.

1 Which of the ideas in the report do you think is best for developing empathy? Why?

2 Why is empathy important in life?

Explore it!

Guess the correct answer.

Which of these can make you happier?

a smelling flowers
b the colour yellow
c being outside

Find another interesting fact about happiness. Write a question for your partner to answer.

OWN IT! The Culture Project Teacher's Resource Bank

7 REVIEW

VOCABULARY

1 Circle the correct words.

Hi Lee,

How's it going? I've been in Turkey for a month. I'm [1]*glad / hopeful* I came to a town and not a city. It's more [2]*peaceful / grateful*. I've been practising Turkish a lot – you know me, I'm [3]*eager / insecure* to learn! I felt [4]*satisfied / ridiculous* at first, but I'm improving. I'm [5]*thrilled / annoyed* when people understand me, although sometimes people are [6]*hurt / amused* by my mistakes. Mehmet has introduced me to lots of people. I'm really [7]*grateful / down* to him.

Anyway, how are you? Write soon!

James

2 Complete the sentences with an expression with *heart* or *mind*.

1 I'm ______________ about the party. Should I go or not?
2 Waiter! I've ______________ . I'll have pizza, not pasta.
3 My sister's great at ______________ all sorts of facts and dates ______________ .
4 Pollution is an issue that's really ______________ . That's why I don't drive.
5 It takes me ages ______________ what to wear in the morning. I'd prefer a school uniform!
6 Can I talk to you? I've got ______________ . It's about my best friend.

LANGUAGE IN ACTION

3 Complete the sentences with the gerund or infinitive with *to* form of the verbs in brackets.

1 I'm not shy about ________ (give) presentations.
2 I was so glad ________ (see) my cousin at the party.
3 I remember ________ (feel) really insecure on my first day at school.
4 My baby brother is always amused at something. He never stops ________ (laugh).
5 ________ (keep) notes of new vocabulary is really important when you study.

4 Complete the dialogue with the correct subject and object questions.

EMMA Happy birthday!
YUSUF Thanks, guys! This is amazing. Who [1]__________ (cook) the cake?
TIM Emma did.
YUSUF It's delicious. What [2]__________ (put/you) in it, Emma?
EMMA Sorry – that's a secret! Anyway, what [3]__________ (think) of your birthday playlist?
YUSUF I love it. Who [4]__________ (make) it?
TIM Emma put it together.
YUSUF Who [5]__________ (choose) the song that's playing now? It's one of my favourites.
TIM That was me!
EMMA So tell us – what presents [6]__________ (get/you)?
YUSUF Some clothes and this fidget spinner.
TIM Who [7]__________ (give) you that?
YUSUF My cousin. He knows I collect them.
TIM What [8]__________ (want/you) to drink? Some juice, some cola? We've got everything.

Self-assessment

- I can use adjectives to talk about feelings.
- I can use expressions with *heart* and *mind*.
- I can use gerunds and infinitives.
- I can use subject and object questions.

LEARN TO ... GIVE YOUR PARTNER USEFUL FEEDBACK

You can help your partner to improve their speaking by giving useful feedback. When you work together, they can help you improve too.

1 Match 1–5 with a–e to complete advice about giving feedback.

Giving your partner feedback can help them speak, but there are some important things to bear in mind.

1 Being positive is important, so always tell your partner ____
2 You don't want your partner to feel hurt, so ____
3 Remember to focus on their English and avoid ____
4 Feedback should be useful, so don't forget ____
5 Be honest. Don't say something is ____

a talking about personal things.
b to give ideas for how your partner can improve.
c talk about anything negative in a friendly way.
d better or worse than it really is.
e what you liked and what they did well.

2 **Look at the feedback that seven students have given Lars. Do they follow the advice in Exercise 1? Why? / Why not?**

1 *You didn't speak very clearly. You sounded like a robot!*

2 *I'm glad you used lots of the new vocabulary. That was nice!*

3 *You've got a gorgeous voice!*

4 *You repeated some words a lot. I would recommend using synonyms next time.*

5 *You made some grammar mistakes, but maybe because you were nervous.*

6 *That was absolutely the most dreadful presentation in history!*

7 *I think you'll sound more natural next time if you don't learn everything by heart.*

3 **Prepare a talk about a topic in the box.**

a happy memory
growth mindset
how to deal with exam stress
how to stay happy

OWN IT!

4 **Take turns to give your talks. While your partner is speaking, think about these things.**

- What do you like about their talk?
- What language do they use well?
- How can they improve next time?

5 **Give your partner useful feedback using the advice in Exercise 1. Is your partner's feedback on your own talk useful? How?**

8 ADVERTISING

LEARNING OUTCOMES

I can ...

- understand texts about online advertising and social media influencers
- recommend an online tool
- write an online product review
- understand how to use defining and non-defining relative clauses, and indefinite, reflexive and reciprocal pronouns
- talk about advertising and use Internet verbs
- understand word building (nouns and verbs) and how to answer open-ended questions
- create an advert storyboard.

Start it!

1 Look at the photo. Is there a place where you live where you can see lots of adverts like this?
2 Before you watch, think of all the different places where you can see adverts.
3 What are the four important aspects of advertising? Watch and check.
4 What's your favourite advert? Why?

Watch video 8.1

p97

Language in action 8.2

p99

Language in action 8.3

p100

Everyday English 8.4

VOCABULARY
Advertising

8.01 **1 Read the story of an advert and put pictures A–F in the correct order. Listen and repeat the words in bold.**

1 ___ 2 ___ 3 ___
4 ___ 5 ___ 6 ___

8.02 **2 Circle the correct words. Listen and check.**

1 I love watching funny *marketing companies / adverts* online or on TV.
2 My dad always buys the same *brand / product* of toothpaste.
3 Sometimes it's not easy for *sellers / buyers* to decide which product they want.
4 I always look at *ad blockers / reviews* before I buy something new.
5 That advert *advertised / influenced* my decision to buy a new tablet.
6 At school we have to draw a simple design for a *logo / slogan* competition.

ADVERTISING A PRODUCT

First, a company makes something to sell. This is the **product**. Then, they create a **brand** to represent the product – this is a name and design that creates a product's identity. It is usually represented by a symbol or **logo**. There is often a **slogan** (a short phrase that is easy to remember) linked to a brand.

Next an **advert** is made to **advertise** the product. This could be a poster in the street or a short film on the television or online that shows what the product is like. It is made by a **marketing company** to encourage or **influence** people to buy the product.

When the product goes on sale the customer or **buyer** buys the product from a **seller**. Buyers sometimes write their opinions about the product in an online **review**. People who don't want to see online adverts use an **ad blocker**, a computer programme that stops adverts appearing on the screen.

LEARN TO LEARN
Wordbuilding: nouns and verbs

When you learn a noun, check the verb form and record them in a table.

3 Complete the table.

Noun	Verb
advert	1 advertise
product	2
3	buy
review	4
5	block (an ad)
6	market
influencer	7
seller	8

4 Close your books. One person says a noun from the table and the other says the matching verb.

Use it!

5 Read the questions and make notes.

1 Do you think ad blockers are a good idea? Why?
2 Do online reviews influence people to buy a product?
3 Which brand slogans or logos can you remember?

6 Ask and answer the questions in Exercise 5.

Explore it!

Guess the correct answer.

When you see a glass of milk in an advert, it probably isn't milk. What is it?

a paint b glue c yoghurt

Find out some tricks that are used in adverts to make products look good. Write a question for your partner to answer.

READING

A report

1 What can you see in the photos? What do you think people do with the videos? Read the report and check your ideas. (8.03)

2 Read the report again. What do the numbers refer to?

1 31% ______
2 74% ______
3 +600 million ______

3 Which type of advertising do the sentences refer to: *I* (influencer, *UGC* (user-generated content) or *N* (native)?

1 Customers can win prizes. ___
2 Customers share photos of themselves. ___
3 It doesn't look like advertising. ___
4 People buy the products to copy someone else. ___
5 Products are promoted by famous people. ___
6 There is a word that tells you it's an advert. ___

4 Find words in the report that mean:

1 people who follow someone online (I) ______
2 a planned series of activities to advertise a product (UGC) ______
3 something that has your name on (UGC) ______
4 to stop (N) ______
5 paid advertising (N) ______

Voice it!

5 Discuss the questions.

1 Do you have a favourite social media influencer or vlogger?
2 Where have you seen native ads on social media?

Online advertising

Social media influencers

One of the most successful types of advertising on social media is influencer advertising. Brands choose social media stars who have thousands of followers on their blog, YouTube channel or Instagram to advertise their products. The stars talk positively about the products in a natural, personal way, which is different to the slogans in traditional adverts. They might talk about a beauty product, play a song, or wear certain clothes in their videos, photos or blogs. Many fans, who want to copy their favourite social media stars, go and buy the same products when they see them.

What influences us to buy a product?
Shop websites – 56%, Brand websites – 34%, Blogs – 31%

User-generated content

Another technique used is user-generated content, or UGC. You may know a soft drinks company whose advertising campaign put everyday names on their drinks bottles. Buyers took photos of themselves with their personalised bottle and shared them on social media. With UGC the buyer becomes the person who advertises the brand so, for example, they upload photos of themselves wearing clothes with the brand logo. Sometimes companies have competitions where you can win a prize for the best photo, and of course, it's free advertising for the brand.

Who gives you the best product information?
(Traditional media) TV – 34%, radio – 37%, newspapers – 44%,
(UGC) social networking – 50%, reviews – 68%, conversations with friends – 74%

Native advertising

Have you ever used an ad blocker so you don't see so many adverts online? Ad blockers block some adverts, but not native advertising. It's a type of advertising that you can't see because it looks exactly the same as a social platform or website. For example, on Facebook a native ad looks like a normal post with like, share and comment buttons, or it could be a photo or video on Instagram. However, if you look closely, you will see the words 'sponsored' or 'paid post' next to it. The good thing about native advertising is that users don't feel like their favourite social media channels are full of adverts, but some people don't like the idea of hidden adverts.

Fact: +600M people use ad blockers

Pronunciation p142

Finished? p125 Ex 1

LANGUAGE IN ACTION

Defining and non-defining relative clauses

Watch video 8.2
What is he giving advice about?
What should you do with your phone?

Defining relative clauses
With UGC the buyer becomes the person [1] ________ / **that** advertises the brand.
It's a type of advertising **which** / [2] ________ you can't see.
Sometimes companies have competitions [3] ________ you can win a prize for the best photo.
Many fans buy the same products [4] ________ they see them.
You may know a soft drinks company [5] ________ advertising campaign put everyday names on their drinks bottles.
Non-defining relative clauses
The stars talk positively about the products in a natural, personal way, [6] ________ is different to the slogans in traditional adverts.
Many fans, [7] ________ want to copy their favourite social media stars, go and buy the same products when they see them.

1 **Complete the examples in the table above. Use the report on page 96 to help you.**

2 **Circle the correct relative pronouns.**

1 The online advertising *who* / *which* most teens prefer is made by social media influencers.
2 Influencers *that* / *whose* channels have the most followers advertise lots of products.
3 Some influencers *who* / *where* advertise products are paid lots of money.
4 Many teens ignore adverts *which* / *when* they see them on social networking sites.
5 Marketing companies look for sites online *which* / *where* they can advertise products.

Use it!

3 **Complete the sentences with the relative pronouns in the box and your own ideas.**

when	which	whose

1 A time ________ I feel happy is ________________.
2 Someone ________ videos I have watched is ________________.
3 The apps ________ I use most are ________________.

4 **Join the two sentences with a relative pronoun.**

1 Jo has got her own vlog. Jo is older than me. (who)
Jo, who's older than me, has got her own vlog.
2 We're going on holiday to the beach. Katia's family have got a house at the beach. (where)
____
3 My phone takes excellent photos. My phone is really old. (which)
____

Use it!

5 **Think of six quiz questions about facts you have read in this book. Use a relative clause.**
What was the name of the person who … ?

6 **Ask and answer your questions.**

Finished? p125 Ex 2

VOCABULARY AND LISTENING

Internet verbs

8.06 **1 Match words 1–10 with definitions a–j. Listen and repeat the words in bold.**

- I [1]**subscribe to** a YouTube channel about parkour. They [2]**post** some awesome videos on it.
- If your Internet doesn't work, [3]**switch** it **off** and then [4]**switch** it **on** again.
- My sister didn't [5]**build up** many followers on Twitter so she [6]**shut down** her account.
- You should [7]**follow** Zoella. She [8]**vlogs** about loads of interesting things and I love her recipes.
- If people [9]**comment on** the post and it isn't very nice, we [10]**delete** it.

a choose to see the things someone uploads on social media 7
b close or stop something ☐
c increase the number of something ☐
d make and share videos online ☐
e put a message or image on social media ☐
f remove something ☐
g start something working ☐
h stop something working ☐
i write your opinion online ☐
j agree to regularly receive an online service or information about it ☐

Use it!

2 Ask and answer questions. Find three things you have in common.

commented on something	deleted something
followed someone	posted something
subscribed to a channel	vlogged about something

Have you ever followed someone on social media?

Yes, of course!

Who do you follow?

I follow all my friends and some celebrities online.

An interview

8.07 **3 Jerome is an influencer. Put the events in the order you think he did them. Listen to the interview and check your answers.**

a He tried out and reviewed products. ☐
b He commented on other posts. ☐
c He got 10,000 followers. ☐
d He posted videos every day. ☐
e He set up his own YouTube channel. ☐

LEARN TO LEARN

Open-ended questions

Read open-ended questions before you listen and think of possible answers. As you listen, make notes of important words, (names, numbers, etc.).

4 Discuss the questions in Exercise 5. Think of possible answers for each question.

Jerome wanted to talk about a hobby, teach people about something or show people how to make something.

8.07 **5 Listen again and answer the questions.**

1 Why did Jerome start a YouTube channel?
Because he wanted to talk about gaming.
2 Why did he delete his videos at first?
____
3 What did his followers like about his vlogs?
____
4 Why did he nearly shut down his account?
____
5 How did he solve the problem?
____
6 When did companies send him new games?
____
7 What advice does he give?
____

6 Would you like to be an influencer? Why? / Why not?

LANGUAGE IN ACTION

Indefinite, reflexive and reciprocal pronouns

Indefinite pronouns
Give your followers **something** new.
No one is interested in your selfies.
Have you got any advice for **anyone**?
There weren't any comments from [1] ________ .
I think that's why **everyone** likes it so much.
Reflexive pronouns
I tried the game out **myself**.
People are interested in [2] ________ .
Reciprocal pronouns
Some followers started arguing with **each other** / **one another**.

Get it right!

*They looked at **themselves** in the mirror.*
(Each person looked at himself/herself.)
*They looked at **each other**.*
(They looked at the different people in the group.)

1 **Complete the examples in the table above.**

2 **Circle the correct indefinite pronouns.**

1 Has *anybody* / *nobody* seen this funny video?
2 I've looked *everywhere* / *somewhere* for my mobile, but I can't find it *anywhere* / *somewhere*.
3 *Anyone* / *No one* commented on *anything* / *everything* she said.
4 We're going *everywhere* / *somewhere* in the centre of town for *everything* / *something* to eat.
5 Are you doing *anything* / *everything* special for your birthday?

3 **Complete the sentences with reflexive pronouns.**

1 She taught ________ how to set up a website.
2 We really enjoyed ________ at the party.
3 He's selfish. He only thinks about ________ .
4 I love taking selfies of ________ .

Watch video 8.3
How many followers do micro-influencers have? Why are they better than celebrity influencers?

4 **Match 1–4 with a–d. Then make sentences with *each other* / *one another*.**

1 My brother lives in the USA so we talk to
2 We talk a lot. We're always sending
3 We haven't seen
4 They don't understand

a and argue all the time.
b for ages.
c messages.
d with a webcam.

1 *My brother lives in the USA so we talk to each other / one another with a webcam.*
2 ________
3 ________
4 ________

8.08 **5** **Circle the correct words to complete the text. Listen and check.**

Ads are [1] *everywhere* / *anywhere*, but have you ever asked [2] *ourself* / *yourself* how advertising works? Marketing companies use techniques to make us buy things we don't even want. [3] *Everything* / *Nothing* is more effective than making us think that we are missing out on [4] *something* / *anything* that [5] *everyone* / *no one* else has and that we will be happier if we buy [6] *ourselves* / *themselves* something new. They also make us compare [7] *myself* / *ourselves* to others. For example, in a typical shampoo ad, two women look at [8] *themselves* / *each other*. One of them asks herself, 'Why is her hair so beautiful?' When they talk to [9] *one another* / *themselves* she discovers the secret: The incredible shampoo!

Use it!

6 **Complete the sentences so they are true for you.**

1 I have taught myself to ________ .
2 I never go anywhere without ________ .

Finished? p125 Ex 3

SPEAKING

Recommending an online tool

8.09 **1** **Listen to the conversation. What problem does Niall have? What does Ginny recommend?**

8.09 **2** **Complete the conversation with the phrases from the *Useful language* box. Listen and check.**

GINNY What's up, Niall?

NIALL I've got to make a video for my technology project to advertise something and I don't have a clue what to do. [1] *I don't know where to start* ! Can you think of anything?

GINNY [2] ________ use a video creation tool. [3] ________ to make videos. I've used some great ones. There are loads of options online.

NIALL That sounds like a plan. What do I need to know?

GINNY Well, a video creation tool [4] ________ because it would provide you with a ready-made template.

NIALL [5] ________ ?

GINNY Yeah, you can teach yourself to do it, no problem.

NIALL Excellent! So I add my own text and images, do I?

GINNY Well, you need to write your own text, but most video creation tools have a ready-made image bank, which is handy.

NIALL Great, I can use their images.

GINNY Yep and you can add music and a voiceover. [6] ________ !

NIALL Sounds like a no-brainer. I'll check out the options online. Thanks, Ginny!

Useful language

I can't recommend it/them enough!

I don't know where to start!

Is it easy to use?

It's the best thing …

(It) would be ideal …

You really ought to …

3 **Match the *Everyday English* phrases with the meanings 1–4. How do you say these phrases in your language?**

1 useful ________

2 I have no idea. ________

3 What's the matter? / How are you? ________

4 obviously the right choice ________

Watch video 8.4
Everyday English

handy I don't have a clue. no-brainer What's up?

PLAN

4 **Make notes about an online tool you want to recommend. Use the ideas below or your own ideas.**

an app a comic maker a music video creator a presentation tool

____

____

____

SPEAK

5 **Practise recommending the tool to your partner. Remember to use language from this unit and phrases from the *Useful language* and *Everyday English* boxes.**

CHECK

6 **Work with another pair. Listen to their conversation and complete the notes.**

What tool did they talk about? ________

____

Did they give a good recommendation? ________

____

HOME | STORIES | PHOTOS

Star rating ★★★★★

1 ☐ ***Sounds Around*** is a great new product. If you're looking for a wireless speaker with a cool design, which is compact in size but big in sound quality, this is for you.

2 ☐ ***Sounds Around*** is designed to be used outside. You can take it everywhere, to the beach, camping or to a pool party. It has all the features you need, it looks great and is extremely tough. One of its best features is that it's waterproof. It also allows you to connect two devices at the same time, so you can choose to play music from either of them. The charging cable is included, but the one thing that's missing is a microphone, so you can't record yourself. However, the battery lasts for 10 hours, which is more than other wireless speakers offered by other brands.

3 ☐ ***Sounds Around*** offers the buyer an excellent range of features at an amazing price. In my opinion it's one of the best low-cost speakers. I can't recommend it enough!

WRITING

An online product review

1 Look at the picture. Which of the features in the box do you think the speaker has? Read the review and check.

compact size · good price · good sound · lightweight · long-lasting battery · microphone · waterproof · wireless

2 Read the review again. Match titles a–c with paragraphs 1–3.

a Opinion
b Short description of the product
c Design and specific features

3 Discuss the questions.

1 Where does the reviewer suggest taking the speaker?
2 What's the advantage of connecting to two devices at the same time?
3 What doesn't the reviewer like about the speaker?
4 Why is the battery better than that of other brands?

4 Read the review again and complete the phrases in the *Useful language* box.

Useful language

[1] ______ is included. It allows you to [2] ______
It is designed to be used [3] ______
One of its best features is [4] ______
The one thing that's missing is [5] ______

Write your own online product review.

PLAN

5 Choose a product to review. Make notes.

short description of the product
design and specific features
your opinion

WRITE

6 Write your product review. Remember to include three paragraphs, language from this unit and phrases from the *Useful language* box.

CHECK

7 Do you …

- give a star rating?
- say what you like and don't like?
- say whether you would buy it?

Finished? p125 Ex 4

THE ART AND DESIGN PROJECT

An advert storyboard

1 **Look at the pictures from an advert. What product does it advertise?**

8.10 2 **Work in pairs. Look at the pictures and guess the dialogue for each one. Listen and check.**

8.10 3 **Listen again and complete the table.**

Advert features	Example
1 What's the problem?	*Katia has a backpack that isn't waterproof. When it rains everything gets wet.*
2 What's the solution?	
3 What are the special features of the product?	
4 Who are the characters in the story?	
5 What information does the narrator give?	
6 What's the slogan?	

How to give feedback

4 **Feedback should be positive and useful. Complete the feedback phrases with the words in the box.**

best how idea maybe positive work

The thing I liked [1] ________ was …
Some [2] ________ things were …
I really liked [3] ________ you …
… is a great [4] ________ .
[5] ________ you could …
… might [6] ________ too.

A

C

B

D

PLAN

5 Work in groups. Choose a product from the box or your own idea.

sunglasses with headphones personalised trainers a new flavour of soft drink a new perfume

Make a list of its features and the good things about its design. Then create an advert storyboard to advertise the product. Complete the steps below.

- Copy the table in Exercise 3 and complete it with information about your product.
- Write a dialogue and narrator's voiceover.
- Decide how to present the storyboard (act it out, video, poster, slide presentation).
- Work together to prepare your storyboard.
- Practise your presentation.

PRESENT

6 Present your storyboard to your classmates. Remember to use information in Exercises 3 and 5.

CHECK

7 Look at your classmates' storyboard presentations. Give them motivating feedback with the phrases in the *How to* give feedback section. Which advert is your favourite?

8 REVIEW

VOCABULARY

1 Complete the advertising facts with the words in the box.

ad blocker advert advertise brand buyer influence logo marketing company product review seller slogan

Advertising facts

An [1] ________ or ad is a short film, song or picture that tries to make you buy a [2] ________.

When you [3] ________ something you tell people about it to try to sell it.

A [4] ________ is the name you call a product. It is often represented by a symbol or [5] ________.

A [6] ________ buys something from a [7] ________. They sometimes give their opinions about the product in a [8] ________.

When you [9] ________ someone, you change how they think about something.

An [10] ________ is a computer programme that stops adverts appearing on screen.

A [11] ________ is a business that encourages people to buy things.

A [12] ________ is a short phrase used in an advert that is easy to remember.

2 Circle the correct words.

1 Are you going to *post* / *vlog* those photos online?
2 If you don't like comments, you can *subscribe to* / *delete* them.
3 How many people do you *build up* / *follow* online?
4 We have to *switch off* / *shut down* our phones at school.

LANGUAGE IN ACTION

3 Join the sentences to make one sentence with a defining or non-defining relative clause.

1 Pablo is Eva's cousin. Pablo does voiceovers.
____
2 She lent me a book. It didn't have the last page.
____
3 The film was about Corfu. We went to Corfu on holiday.
____
4 Ali is a friend. His wife is an influencer.
____

4 Complete the comments with the words in the box.

each other everyone everything myself ourselves themselves

1 Sometimes images in ads make me feel bad about ________.
2 When we see an ad, we should tell ________ that it's not the real world.
3 ________ sees adverts, but that doesn't mean they believe ________ they see.
4 Many ads show people enjoying ________.
5 Some online ads encourage users to tell ________ about new products.

Self-assessment

I can use words to talk about advertising.

I can use verbs to talk about the Internet.

I can use defining and non-defining relative clauses.

I can use indefinite, reflexive and reciprocal pronouns.

LEARN TO LEARN

LEARN TO ... WORK OUT THE MEANING OF NEW WORDS

You can work out the meaning of new words and phrases by using clues from the rest of the text.

1 Read the text quickly, ignoring the words in **bold** if you don't understand them. Do you think space advertising is a good idea?

Space advertising

Imagine this. It's 2030 and you're **gazing** up at the night sky. The stars are **twinkling** and the moon is bright, but these days they're **no longer** alone. They've been joined by lots of huge signs in the **darkness**, like the **billboards** you see at the sides of a road, advertising everything from soft drinks to holidays. This might sound like science fiction, but space adverts will be with us **sooner or later**. In fact, a Russian company is already developing the technology to make it possible, and wants to send up its first ads in the next few years.

They will be created by special **satellites**, like the ones that send and receive TV and internet signals, only smaller. These satellites, **arranged** in groups to make the shapes of words or logos, will **reflect** light from the sun and will be **visible** at night from anywhere on Earth. For companies eager to advertise their products to buyers **around the globe**, this might seem like a dream come true. But ask yourself this: shouldn't we keep somewhere free from advertising? After all, ad blockers won't work in space.

2 Three students are working out the meaning of the words in **bold**. Which ones are they talking about?

1 *OK, it's a noun. They must be a kind of advertising sign, because it says you see them at the sides of a road. What else? Well, I know 'board' from 'whiteboard'...*

____

2 *I think this phrase must be about when the ads will be sent up. I know 'soon' and 'late'. They're both about time and they're opposites ...*

____

3 *It's a verb, something that stars do. I think it's connected to their light, because the sentence also says 'and the moon is bright'.*

____

3 What do you think the words mean?

1 ______________
2 ______________
3 ______________

OWN IT!

4 Choose five of the other words or phrases in **bold**. Answer the questions to try to work out their meaning.

1 What is it? A verb, a noun, an adjective or a phrase?
2 What does the rest of the sentence tell you about it?
3 Do you understand part(s) of the word or phrase?
4 What do you think it means?

5 Check the meanings in a dictionary or with your teacher. Were you correct? Did the questions in Exercise 4 help you?

9 HAVE YOU HEARD THE NEWS?

LEARNING OUTCOMES

I can ...

- understand a newspaper story and a news report
- tell an anecdote
- write a news story
- understand how to use reported statements, commands and questions
- use reporting verbs and adverbs of time and manner
- tell stories to remember new verbs, compare notes to improve listening, learn irregular adjective and noun pairs, and practise summarising.

Start it!

1 Look at the photo. What do you think the children are telling each other?
2 Before you watch, why do people like stories?
3 How have Hollywood films and the Internet changed storytelling? Watch and check.
4 Do you like stories with a moral? Why / Why not?

Watch video 9.1

p109

Language in action 9.2

p111

Language in action 9.3

p112

Everyday English 9.4

p114

Globetrotters 9.5

VOCABULARY
Reporting verbs

1 **Read news stories A–D. Which one is most interesting? Why?**

9.01 2 **Match the words in bold in the news stories with definitions (a–l). Listen, check and repeat.**

A A woman in Georgia, USA [1]**claimed** that she had thrown away jewellery worth $100,000 into the rubbish. The rubbish collection company agreed to look through nearly ten tonnes of rubbish to try and find a black bag with the jewellery. After three hours, they [2]**announced** that they had found it.

a told people officially [2]
b said something was true even if it might not be [ ]

B A curator at a university in Australia who [3]**insisted** that he should open an old box in a store room [4]**discovered** that it contained an Egyptian mummy that he believes is 2,500 years old. Experts [5]**have confirmed** that the body is an adult and [6]**suggest** that it might be an important woman from ancient Egyptian society.

c have shown that something is true [ ]
d found something, especially for the first time [ ]
e said something firmly [ ]
f mention an idea for others to consider [ ]

C A family [7]**have complained** that their neighbours have stolen their cat. However, the neighbours [8]**deny** that they stole the cat and say that it was homeless and hungry, so they gave it food and a home. The neighbours say that the family [9]**refuses** to believe that the cat prefers to live with them!

g say something is not true [ ]
h say you will not do something [ ]
i have told someone that something is wrong [ ]

D A school in the north of England [10]**has apologised** for leaving a teenage student in London after a school trip to the capital city. The school [11]**admitted** that they made a mistake and [12]**promised** that it will never happen again.

j agreed that something was true [ ]
k has said sorry for something someone has done [ ]
l told someone you will certainly do something [ ]

LEARN TO LEARN
Telling stories to remember new words

Use reporting verbs in stories to remember what they mean.

3 **Work in pairs.**

Student A: Tell your partner one of the stories in Exercise 1. Use reporting verbs, but change one fact.

Student B: Listen to your partner tell the story. What did they change?

Use it!

4 **Read the options. Make notes on your answers.**

Think of a time when you … something.

1 admitted to ______
2 denied ______
3 promised to do ______
4 apologised for ______
5 refused to do ______

5 **Compare your answers. Which situations were the most difficult? Which were the easiest?**

Explore it!

Guess the correct answer.

In 2014 a French family found a Caravaggio painting in their house. Experts suggested it could be worth … million.

a €20 b €80 c €120

Find an interesting fact about something famous or valuable. Write a question for your partner to answer.

Pronunciation p142

READING

A newspaper story

9.04 **1 Read the newspaper story. Circle the best title.**

a The twins who have never met.

b The twins who have never spent a day apart.

c International twins!

2 Read the newspaper story again and circle the correct answers.

1 Jonas and Santiago have …
  a nothing in common.
  b the same adoptive parents.
  c lots in common.
  d the same school friends.

2 The orphanage … the boys …
  a said … weren't twins.
  b took … to Spain.
  c gave … a blue sweatshirt.
  d suggested … were twins.

3 The twins see each other …
  a every day.
  b as often as possible.
  c only in the USA.
  d only on social media.

4 The boys were filmed …
  a only in Spain.
  b only in the USA.
  c in Spain and the USA.
  d separately.

3 Find words in the story that mean:

1 exactly the same (paragraph 1) ________

2 a home for children whose parents cannot care for them (paragraph 2) ________

3 taken into a different family and looked after (paragraph 2) ________

4 from the same family (paragraph 3) ________

1 **Identical twins Jonas and Santiago look similar, sound similar and even love the same things. But they live separate lives in different parts of the world and very nearly didn't discover that each other existed.**

2 In 2004, Jonas and Santiago were left at an orphanage in Ghana, Africa when they were babies. A few months later both boys were adopted but by different families; Jonas by a couple from New York and Santiago by a Spanish family. Fortunately, both families went to collect their baby son at the adoption agency in Ghana on the same day and both had bought a new blue sweatshirt for him to wear. A woman at the adoption agency suggested that the babies looked extremely similar and when the parents saw the two baby boys together in their blue sweatshirts they agreed that they were exactly the same. The parents then discovered that the boys shared the same birthday, but the orphanage denied that they were twins.

3 The four adoptive parents couldn't believe that the boys weren't related and insisted that they were going to do a DNA test, which confirmed that the boys were in fact identical twins. The parents promised to keep in touch and said that they would meet as soon as they could, which wasn't easy because Santiago lived in a small village in northern Spain and Jonas on the other side of the world in New York.

4 However, in 2010 they finally met and although they couldn't speak the same language, there was a deep connection between the brothers.

A twin 'can understand you when most people don't,' Jonas said. 'Like in weird situations when you feel a certain way, most people are like, 'What?' But your twin is like, 'Oh, yeah. Yeah, I get that.' I am like, 'Thank you, someone finally gets me.'

5 Since then, they have seen each other several times and speak online regularly. In an interview, Jonas explained that he had learned some Spanish phrases, such as how to ask for directions, and that Santiago's English had improved dramatically. In 2012 a Spanish film director offered to make a film to tell the boys' story. He suggested filming the boys together in both Spain and the USA. He told the boys to act naturally while he filmed them, so we get to see the boys playing football in the Spanish countryside and going skateboarding and to the cinema in the USA. Jonas admitted that being in a film was 'a bit strange' but 'really fun', especially with his twin brother by his side.

Voice it!

4 Discuss the questions.

1 What is the most amazing thing about their story?

2 What would be difficult about living in a different country to your twin?

3 What would you ask Jonas or Santiago if you met them?

4 Would you like to be a twin? Why / Why not? (If you are a twin, what do / don't you like about it?)

Finished? p126 Ex 1

LANGUAGE IN ACTION

Reported statements and commands

Watch video 9.2
Why did the visitors to the zoo complain? What did the zoo claim?

Statements
The orphanage **denied** (that) they **were** twins.
The parents **insisted** (that) they [1] ______ **going to do** a DNA test.
The parents **said** (that) they [2] ______ **meet**.
The parents **promised to keep** in touch.
Jonas **explained** (that) Santiago's English [3] ______ **improved** dramatically.
Orders / Commands
He [4] ______ the boys **to act** naturally.
He **told** me **not to worry**.

1 **Complete the examples in the table above. Use the story on page 108 to help you.**

Get it right!

After ***tell***, we use words like *the boys*, *me*, etc. and the *to* infinitive.

*She **told him (not) to go**.*

2 **Circle the correct words.**

The director has agreed [1]*that he makes* / *to make* another film about twins Jonas and Santiago. He explained that the new film [2]*had been* / *would be* about their lives as teenagers and he told us that the boys [3]*were* / *had been* more independent now and that they [4]*were starting* / *to start* to travel between the USA and Spain without their parents. He said that Jonas [5]*lived* / *had been living* with Santiago in Spain and [6]*to go* / *had been* to school with his brother.

3 **Complete the reported statements and commands.**

1 'I'll do my homework when the film has finished.'
He explained that he …
would do his homework when the film had finished.

2 'I'm going to play your song.'
He promised me that he ______

3 'I didn't take my dad's tablet!'
She denied that she ______

4 'Don't watch this video!'
He told me ______

5 'We will come and meet you at the park.'
They said that they ______

Reported offers and suggestions
A Spanish film director **offered** [1] ______ (make) a film to tell the boys' story.
He **suggested** [2] ______ (film) the boys together in both Spain and the USA.

4 **Complete the examples in the table above with the correct form of the verbs in brackets. Use the story on page 108 to help you.**

Use it!

5 **Read the dialogue. Write offers and suggestions in reported speech.**

SOFIA Shall we go to the cinema?
PAULA OK. Let me see what's on.
SOFIA What about *Horror Fair*?
PAULA Sounds good.
SOFIA Shall we go at six o'clock?
PAULA Sure. I can buy the tickets online.

Sofia suggested going to the cinema later.

______

6 **Tell each other the offers and suggestions that Sofia and Paula made.**

Finished? p126 Ex 2

LISTENING AND VOCABULARY

A news report

1 **Look at headlines a–c. What do you think the stories are about?**

a Sock horror in girl's bedroom

b **The bird that came back speaking another language**

c Emergency in the kitchen!

9.05 **2** **Listen and put the stories in Exercise 1 in the order you hear them.**

1 ___ 2 ___ 3 ___

LEARN TO LEARN

Collaborative listening

Talking about what you understood with a partner before listening a second time can help you find out what you missed.

3 **Tell your partner what you remember about each story. Do you remember the same information?**

9.05 **4** **Listen again and answer the questions. Did talking to your partner in Exercise 3 help you?**

1 Where had the parrot been?

____

2 Why did Darren decide not to keep the parrot after he was found?

____

3 What mistake did the girls make?

____

4 What was the emergency?

____

5 Why did the English family make a phone call?

____

6 Why didn't the specialist touch the 'lizard' immediately?

____

Adverbs of time and manner

5 **Read the blog. Which of the two news stories in the blog do you think was invented?**

If you read my blog **regularly**, you'll know I **occasionally** write about 'unbelievable' news stories, like the one about the parrot that spoke Spanish **fluently**. **Nowadays**, there's so much information on the Internet that it's difficult to know if something is true or not. The other day, I was reading a story about a boy who had invented a robot to do his homework. It said he'd been **secretly** developing the technology in his bedroom, **patiently** trying out different designs. Cool idea, right? But the story got **gradually** more ridiculous. It said that one day the robot had offered to go to school, telling the boy he could stay in bed. **After a while**, I began to think, 'This can't be true.' **Eventually**, I realised it was a joke. It's **surprisingly** easy to believe 'fake news'!

9.06 **6** **Match the adverbs in bold in the blog with their definitions. Listen, check and repeat.**

1 little by little *gradually* [M]

2 these days ________ [ ]

3 sometimes but not often ________ [ ]

4 in the end ________ [ ]

5 in an unexpected way ________ [ ]

6 without telling anyone ________ [ ]

7 often ________ [ ]

8 in a patient way ________ [ ]

9 easily and well ________ [ ]

10 after some time ________ [ ]

7 **Are the adverbs in Exercise 6 adverbs of time (*T*) or manner (*M*)?**

Use it!

8 **Think of situations when people do things in these ways. Can your partner guess the verb and adverb?**

gradually: get better, move

regularly: go to bed late, not eat, practise

patiently: listen, sit, wait

secretly: gesture, speak, write

This happens before you play an important football match.

You practise regularly?

Yes!

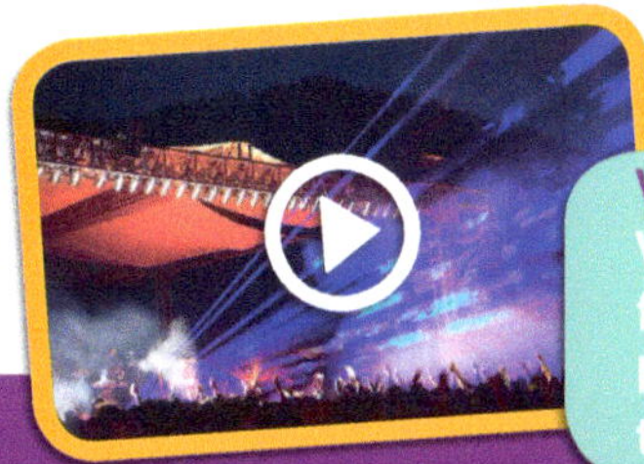

Watch video 9.3
What did the two friends want to see?
How did they get into the radio studio?

LANGUAGE IN ACTION

Reported questions

Direct questions	Reported questions
***Wh-* questions**	
'What **are** your favourite stories?'	Last week, one of our listeners asked us [1] ______ our favourite stories **were**.
'Where **did** you **leave** the other sock?'	Everybody asked her [2] ______ she**'d left** the other sock.
***Yes/No* questions**	
'**Can** we have the parrot back?'	The Guatemalan family asked Darren if they **could** have the parrot back.
'**Have** you ever **cooked** anything before?'	Their Italian friends asked them [3] ______ they**'d** ever **cooked** anything before.

1 **Complete the examples in the table above.**

9.07 **2** **Put the words in the correct order to make sentences. Listen and check.**

1. the boy / had / his homework / done / the teacher / if / asked / he
   The teacher asked the boy if he had done his homework.
2. doing / Laura / what / she / Jack / later / asked / was
   ______
3. me / ended / asked / my sister / how / the story / had
   ______
4. left / the assistant / any tickets / were / I / there / asked / if /
   ______
5. we / where / the station / an old man / was / asked
   ______
6. arrive / Tom / me / would / I / asked / what time
   ______

9.08 **3** **Rewrite the sentences as reported questions. Listen and check.**

1. 'Who's the hero of the story?' Mikhail asked his sister.
   Mikhail asked his sister who the hero of the story was.
2. 'Do you prefer comedy or drama?' Elena asked me.
   ______
3. Ruben asked his friend, 'Where did you hear that?'
   ______
4. 'Will it rain later?' she asked.
   ______
5. 'Can we still get tickets?' I asked the receptionist.
   ______
6. 'What are you reading?' Sally asked me.
   ______

Use it!

4 **Think of five questions someone asked you last week. Write the names and tell your partner the questions. Can they guess who asked what?**

my maths teacher, my dad, my best friend Rachel, my sister, my cousin.

This person asked me if I had cleaned my room.

Your dad asked you if you had cleaned your room.

No, try again!

______

Finished? p126 Ex 3

SPEAKING

Telling an anecdote

9.09 **1** **Look at the photo. What happened at the bowling alley? Listen to the conversation and check.**

9.09 **2** **Complete the conversation with the phrases from the *Useful language* box. Listen and check.**

JAMIE [1] You'll never guess what happened to me last night.
ESMA No, what? Tell me.
JAMIE [2] ________________ embarrassing! [3] ________________ was, my new classmates asked me if I wanted to go bowling with them. I said yes and when we got there, they asked me how well I could bowl.
ESMA You didn't say you were any good, did you?
JAMIE Well, you know I'm a show-off! So I said, 'Just watch me!'
ESMA But you're terrible at bowling! I've seen you.
JAMIE Hey! I'm not that bad! So [4] ________________, I picked up the ball, put my fingers in the holes, went to bowl …
ESMA Let me guess. Your fingers got stuck.
JAMIE Completely! I swung the ball back carefully and then swung it forward and just sort of went flying with it. The next [5] ________________, I was flat on my back!
ESMA What a fantastic first impression!
JAMIE And to make matters worse, I couldn't get my fingers out.
ESMA Oh, Jamie!

Useful language

Basically, what happened was …
It was so (+ *adjective*)
So anyway, …
The next thing I knew …
You'll never guess what happened …

Watch video 9.4
Everyday English

Hey! Let me guess.
show-off sort of to make matters worse

3 **Match the words in the *Everyday English* box with the words and phrases 1–5.**

1 I disagree! __________
2 to make the situation even more unpleasant __________
3 someone who tries to make other people look at them __________
4 in a way __________
5 I think I know what you're going to say. __________

PLAN

4 **Make notes on something embarrassing, funny, etc. that has happened to you.**

Introduce the anecdote
Decide which details are the most important
End the anecdote

SPEAK

5 **Practise telling the anecdote to your partner. Remember to use reported statements, commands and questions, vocabulary from this unit and phrases from the *Useful language* and *Everyday English* boxes.**

CHECK

6 **Work with another pair. Listen to their conversation and complete the notes.**

What kind of anecdote was it? __________

What were the important details? __________

How did the anecdote end? __________

Free ice cream, anyone?

Most of us expect to receive presents on our birthday. However, Jimmy Teng or 'Uncle Jimmy' is different. The ice cream man from Singapore regularly gives away free ice cream on his birthday. He started the tradition on his 70th birthday when he offered to give away 700 free ice creams.

This year Uncle Jimmy announced that he was going to give away 1,000 free ice creams. Surprisingly, some customers insisted that they would pay for the ice cream. When asked why he did it, Mr Teng explained that nowadays everyone in Singapore was stressed and he wanted to make them feel happy. He also admitted that sharing ice cream made him feel good too. 'I'm so happy,' he said. 'I wouldn't be this happy if I won the lottery!'

Uncle Jimmy, who has been an ice cream man for over 15 years, has lots of customers. When asked what his favourite flavour was, he answered 'Sweetcorn' and he explained that ice cream in Singapore was sometimes served with bread rather than a cone.

WRITING

A news story

1 **Why would someone give away free ice cream? Read the news story and check.**

2 **Read the news story again and answer the questions.**

1 Who is the story about? ____________

2 What happens? ____________

3 When does it happen? ____________

3 **Discuss the questions about the structure of the story.**

1 What does the headline tell us about the story? What doesn't it tell us?

2 What is the aim of the first sentence?

3 What do we learn in the first paragraph of the story?

4 When do we learn why the story happened?

5 Is the information in the third paragraph necessary or extra?

6 What effect does the direct speech have in the story?

4 **Complete the phrases in the *Useful language* box with details from the news story.**

Useful language

A man from [1] Singapore regularly gives away free ice cream…

He announced/explained/admitted that [2] ____________

[3] '____________,' he said.

Surprisingly/Nowadays etc., [4] ____________

When asked … he answered/explained/said [5] ____________

Write your own news story.

PLAN

5 **Make notes on something special that someone has done to celebrate their birthday or find an interesting news story online.**

WRITE

6 **Write a news story about your idea in Exercise 5. Remember to include three paragraphs, language from this unit and phrases from the *Useful language* box.**

CHECK

7 **Do you …**

- include an interesting headline?
- include some extra details in the third paragraph?
- include some direct speech?

Finished? p126 Ex 4

AROUND THE WORLD

Globetrotters

Watch video 9.5
Stories on stage

- Where do you think opera comes from? Where is it popular?
- What is *jingju* and what does it involve?
- What different skills do *jingju* performers need to have?

READING
A story

1 **Look at pictures A–D. What is happening in each one? Put them in order to make a story.**

9.10 **2** **Were your ideas correct? Read the introduction about Maori storytelling and the story 'How Maui slowed the Sun'.**

3 **Read the introduction and the story again. Write *T* (true) or *F* (false).**

1. The Maori have always written down their stories. F
2. It was impossible for the villagers to finish their work each day. ___
3. Maui had never done anything impressive before. ___
4. Only Maui's brothers helped to make the ropes. ___
5. The Sun saw Maui and his brothers coming closer. ___
6. Maui hit the Sun more than once with the bone. ___
7. The Sun stopped moving completely. ___

MAORI STORYTELLING

Storytelling is an essential part of the culture of the Maori people, the first inhabitants of Aotearoa (New Zealand). They didn't use to have a written language, so they learned stories by heart to remember their history. The Maori people still tell their stories, often in a traditional meeting place called a **marae**. ***The stories are accompanied by dance, songs and chants. Here is one for you to enjoy.***

How Maui slowed the Sun

Long ago, the Sun used to move so quickly across the sky that the days were too short for people in the village to do all their work. The villager Maui, however, had a plan. He gathered his four brothers and said, 'Why should the Sun control us? Let's catch him and make him go more slowly.'

The brothers were worried. They asked Maui if it was really possible to get safely near the Sun. 'The heat and flames will burn us!' they said. 'We might die!' Maui held his grandfather's bone high, and said, 'I have achieved many things which you thought were impossible. I have brought fire to the people, I have caught the greatest fish in the world. With this bone, and with your help, I will catch the Sun.'

Everyone agreed to help him. Over the next five days they made strong ropes to catch the Sun. When they were ready, the brothers set off to the east, where the Sun rises. They travelled during the night so that the Sun wouldn't see them approaching. Eventually, they arrived at an enormous deep hole in the ground. This was where the Sun slept.

While the Sun was still asleep, the brothers built a wall around the hole and hid behind it, waiting patiently. Maui told his brothers not to throw the ropes until he said so. After a while, the ground began to shake. The Sun was waking up! First came his burning hair, then his fiery eyes and his white-hot teeth.

C

D

'Now!' cried Maui. The brothers threw the ropes over the Sun. They tangled in his hair and trapped his huge, hot body. The men pulled on the ropes as strongly as they could.

'What are you doing?' the Sun cried angrily.

Maui jumped on the wall and lifted up his grandfather's bone. He smashed it with all his strength down on the head of the Sun, who screamed in pain.

'Are you trying to kill me?'

'No, but you must go more slowly,' said Maui.

The Sun tried hard to escape, but again and again Maui hit him with the bone. The Sun gradually grew weaker, until at last he could only move slowly across the sky.

And that is why the days are now long enough for all our work, and why sometimes, if you look carefully, you can still see the ropes that connect the Sun to the Earth – shining through the clouds.

LEARN TO LEARN

Irregular adjective and noun pairs

Learn adjectives and their related nouns to increase your vocabulary.

4 **Complete the table with words from the story.**

Adjective	Noun
wide	width
1	height
hot	2
3	length
strong	4
5	depth

Summarising

Sometimes we need to tell a shorter version of a longer story. Summarising can help us to do this.

5 **Put the sentences in order to make a summary of the story.**

a The brothers travelled by night to where the Sun slept. ___
b You can still see the ropes that hold the Sun to the Earth. ___
c Maui hit the Sun with the bone. ___
d Maui, his brothers, and the villagers made strong ropes. ___
e People didn't use to have enough time to do everything because the Sun moved too quickly across the sky. 1
f The Sun eventually started to move more slowly. ___
g When the Sun woke up, the brothers trapped him. ___
h Maui had a plan to control the Sun. ___

Voice it!

6 **Discuss the questions.**

1 Without Maui, could the brothers have trapped the Sun?
2 Talk about a story from your culture. What does it mean?

Explore it!

Guess the correct answer.

Aotearoa, the Maori name for New Zealand, means land of …

a the perfect sky.
b the long white cloud.
c the towering mountains.

OWN IT! The Culture Project Teacher's Resource Bank

9 REVIEW

VOCABULARY

1 Match the reporting verbs in the box with the definitions.

admit	apologise	complain	deny	discover	promise

Which reporting verb do we use to …

1 say that something is not true? ________
2 tell someone you're sorry? ________
3 find out information for the first time? ________
4 agree that something is true? ________
5 tell someone formally something is wrong? ________
6 tell someone you will certainly do something? ________

2 Complete the sentences with the adverbs in the box.

eventually	fluently	gradually	nowadays	regularly	secretly	surprisingly

1 I ________ finished reading the book you recommended but it took me ages.
2 I speak French ________, mostly with my Canadian cousin – once a week.
3 Mike's family planned his birthday party ________. He was very surprised!
4 The exam was ________ easy. I finished it really quickly.
5 My best friend speaks English ________.
6 ________ I get on with my brother, but we didn't use to.
7 My English is improving ________ but I need to learn more vocabulary.

LANGUAGE IN ACTION

3 Complete the second sentences.

1 'I'll help you with your homework.'
Ayaz offered ________
2 'Send me a message when you get there.'
Shaun told me ________
3 'Why don't we meet at the new café?'
Ada suggested ________
4 'I promise I'll give you a lift.'
She promised ________

4 Rewrite the direct questions as reported questions.

1 'Do you often read the news online?' my sister asked me.
____
2 'How can I improve my English?' Zehra asked her teacher.
____
3 'Have you seen what's happened in London?' Ian asked Jake.
____
4 'Will the museum be open tomorrow?' the tourist asked.
____

Self-assessment

I can use reporting verbs.

I can use adverbs of time and manner.

I can use reported statements and commands.

I can use reported questions.

LEARN TO LEARN

LEARN TO ... ASK FOR HELP WHEN YOU DON'T UNDERSTAND

There are different ways to ask English speakers for help and check you understand what they've said.

1 Read the problems people have understanding someone in English. Then discuss the questions.

We asked six language learners what problems they'd had understanding people in English. This is what they told us.

1. For me, it's usually that the other person speaks too fast.
2. The worst thing is when people use lots of difficult words I don't know
3. I usually understand more or less, but I don't understand all of the details.
4. Sometimes I think I've understood someone, but then I realise I haven't at all!
5. My problem is that when I don't understand I'm too shy to say. I just say 'yes' a lot!

Have you had any of these problems? How did you solve them?

2 Read the conversations. Match phrases 1–5 with phrases with similar meanings a–e.

a Could you repeat from the beginning? ___
b I want to make sure I've understood correctly. ___
c What's the meaning of that word? ___
d I didn't hear the last thing you said. ___
e What were your instructions? ___

1

BEN: Sorry, Miss. I didn't understand. [1]**What did you say I had to do?**
TEACHER: I told you to compare the two pictures and discuss how similar they are.
BEN: [2]**What does 'similar' mean?**

2

ALISON: Excuse me, can you tell me how to get to the post office, please?
MAN IN: Sure. Go straight until you see a big building. It's opposite that ...
ALISON: [3]**I didn't catch that.** The big what?
MAN IN: Building.

3

GISELLE: Bea thought Juan had promised he would bring the food, but he hadn't! After a while, someone said-
JO: Wait, wait, wait! [4]**Can you start again, please?** I'm lost!
GISELLE: Sorry, sorry. What happened was that ...

4

VLAD: Which bus do I need for Oxford Park?
WOMAN: You need two, actually. Take the 147 fromhere to Austen Square, cross the road and then take the 29 from in front of the bank.
VLAD: OK, [5]**let me check I've got this right.** First, I take 147 to Austen Square?
WOMAN: That's right.

OWN IT!

3 Student A: choose one of the topics in the box and explain it to Student B. Student B: use the phrases from the conversations in Exercise 2 to help you understand. Then swap roles.

how to get from your school to your house
the story of how Maui slowed the Sun
the rules of a sport

1 FINISHED?

1 Put the letters in order to make words to describe clothes and shoes.

1 

flowery

2 

______

3 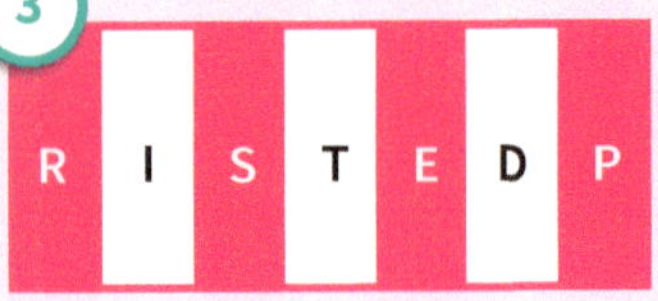

______

4 

______

5 

______

6 

______

7 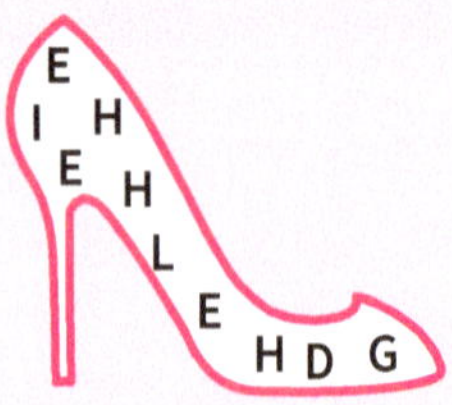

______

8 

______

2 Match the texts with photos a–d.

1 I've just had a totally amazing time! I've been looking at all sorts of interesting animals, with lots of fantastic colours. I haven't done anything like this before, but I'd like to do it again. I've told all my friends, and they want to do it with me next time. ______

2 We've just come back, and we've spent all our money. The good news is now I've got lots of really good clothes, so I don't need to do anything like this again for a long time! ______

3 I've been outside all day, and now I'm feeling pretty tired. I've being doing this since I was very young, and one day, I want to train other people to do the same as me. ______

4 I've had a rather bad experience. I haven't tasted anything so bad for a long time. And since I had it, I've been feeling quite ill. My stomach has been hurting for ages. I'm never going back there, and I'm going to tell all my friends about it!

a 

b 

c 

d 

3 Complete the modifiers with vowels. Make sentences with the modifiers and the words in the box about you.

amazed	better	confused	good at
happier	happy	more interesting	
shocked	slow	slower	taller

1 absolutely
2 _xtr_m_ly
3 r_ _lly
4 t_t_lly
5 f_ _rly
6 pr_tty
7 q_ _t_
8 r_th_r
9 _ l_t
10 _ l_ttl_
11 _ b_t

4 Put the letters in order to make verbs to describe clothes and shoes. Use the letters in the circles to make an expression. Write the mystery expression.

1 WIGOHT GO WITH
2 MTCAH _ _ _ _ _
3 TIF _ _ _
4 WERTAUO _ _ _ _ _ _ _
5 UTSI _ _ _ _
6 HAPNUG _ _ _ _ _ _
7 LOFD _ _ _ _
8 POUD _ _ _ _
9 NODU _ _ _ _

Mystery expression: _ _ _ _ _ _ _ _ _ _ _ _ _ _ _

2 FINISHED?

1 **Read the clues and complete the crossword.**

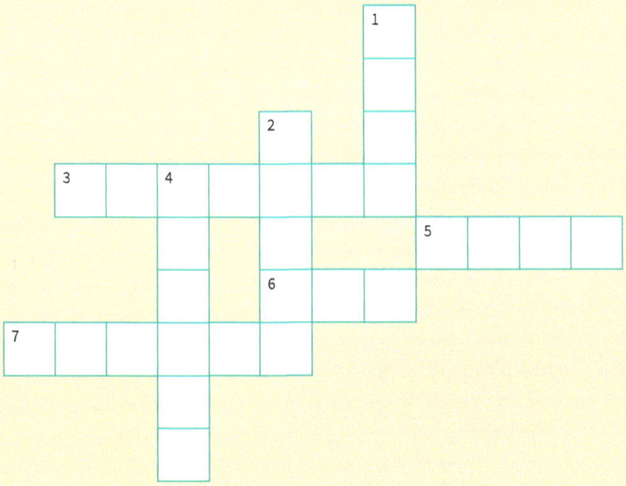

Across

3 I had to do … my phone for a week, because it was broken.

5 Last week, I went … to my old primary school to visit my teacher.

6 I feel bad. I hope I don't … up getting ill.

7 I've … up for piano lessons.

Down

1 I … through a difficult time when I started my new school, but now everything's OK.

2 Sara … out of her old flat, and went to live in a new one.

4 I … down three party invitations last month because I was so busy.

2 **Compare the pictures. How many sentences can you write about Stuart's life in the past with *used to*, *didn't use to* and *would*? Use your imagination!**

When Stuart was a student, he used to live in a flat.

____

____

____

3 **What films had you seen by the time you were ten? Write as many as possible in two minutes.**

4 **Find words in the sentences that rhyme with parts of objects. Change them so the sentences make sense.**

1 Put the ~~kid~~ back or the pen will dry. lid

2 I've broken the sandal on my bag. ________

3 My computer needs a hug. ________

4 The Swiss play on that phone is really bright. ________

5 Don't get the camera pens dirty. ________

6 The map of my bag hurts my shoulder. It's too tight. ________

3 FINISHED?

1 Match the squares to make cooking verbs.

ro	ch	over	gri	sea	pe	sli	fr	ba	spre	gra	he
y	son	te	ke	ll	at	ad	ast	cook	ce	el	op

2 Use the code to write the questions. Answer them so they are true for you.

A = ⚭	B = ☞	C = ■	D = ✘	E = ✈
F = ●	G = ❍	H = ✧	I = ❄	J = ✍
K = ✉	L = ✎	M = ✢	N = ✪	O = ✓
P = ☎	Q = ✾	R = ✇	S = ❑	T = ✐
U = ✳	V = ✶	W = ✂	X = ✆	Y = ✻

1 ✘✓❄✪❍ ✐✧❄❑ ✈✶✈✪❄✪❍
What are you ____________________?
____

2 ❍✓❄✪❍ ✐✓ ✘✓ ✪✈✆✐ ❑✳✢✢✈✇
What are you ____________________?
____

3 ☎✈✓☎✎✈ ✂❄✎✎ ✐✇⚭✶✈✎ ❄✪ ✐✧✈ ●✳✐✳✇✈
How do you think ____________________?
____

4 ✂✈⚭✐✧✈✇ ❍✓❄✪❍ ✐✓ ☞✈ ✎❄✉✈ ✐✓✢✓✇✇✓✂
What's the ____________________?
____

3 Make sentences with the verbs in the box and the future continuous and future perfect.

chat to friends do homework
do sport have dinner
listen to music sleep

At 5 pm I will / won't be …
At 7 pm …
At 11 pm …
By midnight I will / won't have …

____
____
____
____
____
____
____

4 Circle nine more quantities.

H	A	N	D	F	U	L	T	G	F	D
V	Y	D	B	E	H	E	E	D	G	X
S	P	R	I	N	K	L	E	C	C	O
L	K	J	K	C	O	I	C	K	E	W
E	A	S	A	W	U	S	V	I	A	E
E	J	P	D	F	B	P	I	E	C	E
P	Q	O	F	V	S	L	L	C	H	J
O	I	O	V	C	K	A	W	E	U	K
P	J	N	E	D	A	S	I	O	N	R
C	H	F	C	W	Y	H	N	D	K	N
Q	R	U	J	H	Q	B	G	G	R	T
W	S	L	I	C	E	H	T	I	O	M

4 FINISHED?

1 Can you work out these riddles?

1 Sometimes they look like faces, sometimes they look like animals. They're always changing shape. Grey ones usually disappear after the rain.

____

2 It looks like a tear and it tastes a bit like an apple. It sounds the same as two things of the same size that are used together.

____

3 Mine sounds like a bird. Mary's latest one sounds like a famous pop song. We don't know what Dave's sounds like because he always has his mobile on silent.

____

2 Look at the dots. Write four things you think it could be. Join the dots to see if you are right.

It could/might be a ball …

____

____

____

____

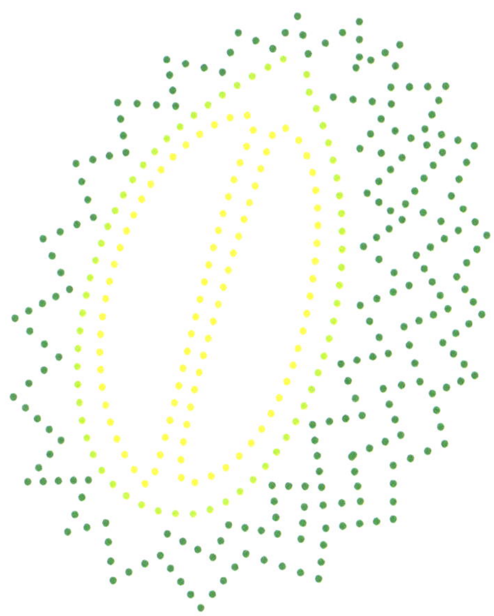

3 Imagine you do an unusual job. Write as many of these as possible in three minutes.

- things you had to do to get your job

- things you have to do every day in your job.

Show your list to a partner. Can they guess the job?

4 Circle nine more adjectives.

R	U	Z	D	H	S	W	I	D	D	T	L
C	O	L	M	S	H	A	R	P	F	R	U
H	G	U	J	T	I	C	Y	L	S	A	F
N	T	X	G	H	N	A	B	U	M	V	R
S	V	O	D	H	Y	L	Q	S	E	U	U
M	K	L	O	D	E	F	E	B	L	H	O
A	I	P	R	M	K	M	U	Z	L	E	L
O	F	H	Z	G	S	P	I	C	Y	F	O
T	A	S	O	U	R	O	W	J	A	C	C
H	D	R	M	V	P	A	S	I	L	J	E
T	N	E	R	A	P	S	N	A	R	T	H
O	S	Q	U	G	A	T	V	Z	N	I	F

5 FINISHED?

1 **Put the letters in order to write two verbs to describe processes.**

1 eodseaptwlev develop waste
2 uclertoplocced ______
3 evaemrrilusede ______
4 lepmtapmnicocsuyu ______
5 toeercaslev ______
6 toctacrenactnt ______

2 **Mark is going to have an operation next week. Complete the sentences about who will be doing what. Put the sentences in order.**

a Next, the anaesthetic ______ (give) by Dr Sanna. ☐
b The second part of the operation ______ (do) by Dr Rees. ☐
c At first, his heart rate ______ (measure) by Nurse Evans. ☐
d Finally, he ______ (take) home by Nurse Simms. ☐
e Until he is completely better, he ______ (visit) in hospital by Dr Jones. ☐
f The first part of the operation ______ (do) by Dr Lansbury. ☐

3 **How many sentences can you write that go in front of these question tags in three minutes?**

1 …, isn't it?
It's freezing today
2 …, doesn't she?
______
3 …, can't they?
______
4 …, would you?
______
5 …, are we?
______
6 …, haven't you?
______
7 …, had he?
______

4 **Circle nine more extreme adjectives.**

F	E	T	D	E	A	F	E	N	I	N	G
R	A	N	E	E	F	R	L	J	A	B	P
E	H	S	O	R	A	F	L	Q	M	O	U
E	D	S	C	R	R	U	I	J	Q	I	N
Z	R	W	T	I	M	I	A	U	J	L	D
I	E	J	J	U	N	O	F	F	I	I	Q
N	A	V	X	X	N	A	U	Y	R	N	B
G	D	V	F	Y	O	N	T	S	I	G	V
D	F	F	C	S	W	I	I	I	K	N	A
B	U	M	L	R	X	N	X	N	N	E	G
V	L	M	A	T	B	T	E	C	G	G	H
M	A	R	V	E	L	L	O	U	S	Z	D
A	B	L	Z	G	O	R	G	E	O	U	S

6 FINISHED?

1 Read the clues and complete the crossword.

Across

2 I always have … with my friends.
5 I get a lot … of my English lessons.
7 We switched off the TV because we got … with the programme.
9 Do you take an … in football?
11 My dad always gets … when he's driving.
12 My grandfather never had the … to go to university.

Down

1 We have 30 minutes before our train arrives, so let's take … of it.
3 My annoying cousin really gets on my … .
4 I have … about whether my team will win tomorrow.
6 My grandmother takes a lot of … in looking at old photos.
8 It's important to take some … in life.
10 I got to … a lot of new people at summer camp last year.

2 Match the jokes with the answers.
Give each joke a score (one star = terrible, five stars = very funny).

1 If you dialled 08968 767 457 454 233 989 767 521 123, what would you get? ___
2 What would happen if you put your music in the fridge? ___
3 What word would become shorter if you added two more letters to it? ___
4 Where would a cow go if it wanted a holiday? ___
5 If you look in any dictionary, which word will always be spelled wrong? ___

e *You'd get some really cool music!* ★★★★★

d *Short!* ☆☆☆☆☆

a **Mooooo York!** ★★★★★

b *A very tired finger!* ☆☆☆☆☆

c **Wrong.** ★★★★★

3 Complete the sentences with third conditional verbs and interesting information to continue the story.

1 If Sara hadn't gone to school that day, she wouldn't have met ________ .
2 If she hadn't met ________ she wouldn't have found out ________ .
3 If she hadn't ____________________________________ .
4 If ____________________________________ .
5 If ____________________________________ .

4 Put the letters in order to make verbs and nouns for inspiration and challenge.

1 a c e e g h l l n *challenge*
2 y e b r a r v ________
3 d t r i a i n o t n m e e ________
4 o p r u i y t n t o p ________
5 b t c e l a s o ________
6 u p r t o p s ________
7 n o r g e a u c e ________
8 o e c m v r o e ________
9 a e c v h e i ________
10 e i n r i s p ________

7 FINISHED?

1 Find the letters and then write them to make the first half of a message. Can you guess the second half?

1. satisfied (letter 2)
2. hopeful (letter 1)
3. peaceful (letter 5)
4. eager (letter 2)
5. glad (letter 2)
6. hurt (letter 4)
7. thrilled (letter 2)
8. annoyed (letter 5)
9. amused (letter 2)
10. ridiculous (letter 4)
11. insecure (letter 2)
12. down (letter 1)

a h _ _ _ _ _ _ _ _ _ _ _ _ is as important as
a _ _ _ _ _ _ _ _ _ _ _ _ _.

2 Four brothers each have a sister who is the complete opposite of them. Match the sentences halves to find out who the sisters are.

Jack keeps eating chocolate all day
Emily avoids eating too much sugar.

Alex never stops	getting up early.
Berat hopes	eating chocolate all day.
Charlie always forgets	to stay in the city forever.
Jacob doesn't mind	talking in class.
Jack keeps	to put his notebook in his bag.

Emily avoids	to get up late every day if she could.
Sara always remembers	to speak during most lessons.
Megan refuses	living in the countryside.
Olivia would love	to take all her books to class.
Mira misses	eating too much sugar.

3 How many pairs of subject and object questions can you write in three minutes using the ideas in the box?

Q: What did Al Zahrawi write?
A: One of the earliest books about medicine.
Q: Who wrote one of the earliest books about medicine?
A: Al Zahrawi.

invent, write, J.K. Rowling, the Ancient Egyptians, build, the iPhone, Steve Jobs, discover, one of the earliest books about medicine, the Italians, gravity, the Pyramids, Isaac Newton, the iPod, the Harry Potter stories, the Pyramids, pizza, Al Zahrawi

4 Put the letters in order and add *heart* or *mind* to make an expression.

yellow: *put my (heart) into*
blue: ______
red: ______
brown: ______
pink: ______
orange: ______
purple: ______
green: ______

	M	T	P	I	T
G	E	U	O	Y	N
S	D	O	L	N	Y
C	H	C	E	E	H
I	S	Y	O	C	M
Y	O	S	M	G	A
S	N	T	N	B	Y
R	O	R	E	L	A
M	T	N	S	R	B
E	I	W	A	O	E
M	E	N	E	'	B
O	A	B	S	M	K
T	I	R	D	O	Y

8 FINISHED?

1 Use the code to complete the questions. Answer them so they are true for you.

A	B	C	D	E	F	G	H	I	J	K	L	M	N	O	P	Q	R	S	T	U	V	W	X	Y	Z
8		24	11	19			12	14		22	17			18			2	26	13	21	6	10		4	

1 W H I C H A D V E R T S D O Y O U L I K E ?
10 12 14 24 12 / 8 11 6 19 2 13 26 / 11 18 / 4 18 21 / 17 14 22 19

2 W _ _ C _ L O _ O _ _ O _ O _ _ _ O W ?
10 12 14 24 12 / 17 18 25 18 26 / 11 18 / 4 18 21 / 22 1 18 10

3 _ O _ O _ E V E _ W _ _ T E _ E V _ E W _ ?
11 18 / 4 18 21 / 19 6 19 2 / 10 2 14 13 19 / 2 19 6 14 19 10 26

4 _ O _ O _ _ _ E A _ _ L O C _ E _ _ ?
11 18 / 4 18 21 / 21 26 19 / 8 11 / 15 17 18 24 22 19 2 26

5 W _ A T _ _ _ L _ E _ C E _ _ O _ T O _ _ _ A _ _ O _ _ C T ?
10 12 8 13 / 14 1 20 17 21 19 1 24 19 26 / 4 18 21 / 13 18 / 15 21 4 / 8 / 23 2 18 11 21 24 13

6 W _ _ C _ _ L O _ A _ _ C A _ _ O _ _ E _ E _ _ E _ ?
10 12 14 24 12 / 26 17 18 25 8 1 26 / 24 8 1 / 4 18 21 / 2 19 16 19 16 15 19 2

2 Complete the sentences with a relative pronoun. Guess what each thing or person is. Use the scrambled words in the box to help you.

1 It's a feeling you have ________ someone has helped you. ________
2 It's a word ________ goes with *have* and means 'a good time'. ________
3 It describes a place ________ you can feel very calm and relaxed. ________
4 It's a word ________ means 'very interesting'. ________
5 It describes someone ________ feels quite angry. ________
6 It's someone ________ products are bought by someone else. ________

lgruafte
unf
lpeuafce
fganisctian
daneyon
relsler

3 Circle five pronouns in the wordsnake. Use them to complete the sentences so they are true for you.

emyselfonboanyonesetsomeoneoranysomethingeverynothingeach

The last time I …
1 enjoyed ________ was ________________.
2 didn't talk to ________ for an hour was ________________.
3 helped ________ was ________________.
4 forgot ________ important was ________________.
5 had ________ to eat and felt hungry was ________________.

4 Circle nine more Internet verbs.

K	W	G	B	I	C	B	K	A	A	N	N	P
S	H	U	T	D	O	W	N	Y	V	K	O	I
O	T	E	B	I	R	C	S	B	U	S	T	W
G	Y	F	S	B	D	R	M	U	N	F	N	O
G	O	N	F	E	U	T	S	O	P	O	E	Q
J	Z	L	L	O	A	I	H	Y	D	L	M	Y
W	S	E	V	E	H	C	L	E	M	L	M	E
Y	T	H	X	X	T	C	H	D	Y	O	O	Y
E	U	S	R	I	X	Q	T	C	U	W	C	Y
E	X	N	W	N	H	L	M	I	Z	P	E	A
E	S	S	T	N	I	R	P	R	W	X	D	B
D	H	X	K	Q	S	H	K	H	X	S	G	C
P	Y	P	W	C	K	R	O	S	U	B	C	F

9 FINISHED?

1 Match the squares to make reporting verbs.

de	apolo	ann	con	com	ad	in	sug	re	pro
plain	mise	ny	ounce	gest	sist	mit	fuse	firm	gise

2 Write examples of the following.

A time when you …

1 suggested doing something different. ______
2 offered to help someone. ______
3 denied that you had done something and then admitted that you had done it. ______
4 promised to do something. ______
5 insisted that you did something. ______
6 told someone to do something. ______

3 Imagine you are a famous athlete, pop star or actor. How many things can you list that you've often been asked by fans in three minutes?

Lionel Messi
My fans have often asked me …
… what my dream team would be.
… if I get nervous before taking a penalty.

4 Complete the sentences with the adverbs in the box. What is the adverb in the boxed letters?

after a while eventually fluently gradually ~~nowadays~~ patiently regularly secretly surprisingly

1 Most people n [o] w a d a y s have a mobile.
2 I whispered _ _ [c] _ _ _ _ _ to her. [c]
3 _ _ _ _ _ [ ] _ _ _ _ _, the baby fell asleep.
4 The twins are _ _ _ _ _ _ [ ] _ _ _ _ _ different.
5 The teacher waited _ _ _ [ ] _ _ _ _ _. [o] [n]
6 The rain _ _ _ _ _ _ [ ] _ _ _ stopped.
7 Aroha spoke Maori _ [ ] _ _ _ _ _ _ _.
8 English gets _ _ _ _ _ _ _ [ ] _ _ easier.
9 The Olympics take place _ _ _ _ _ _ _ _ [ ].

STARTER VOCABULARY BANK

Travel

accommodation

backpacking

holiday resort

sightseeing

tourist attraction

trip

Music and theatre

audience	part	scene
lines	rehearsal	show

1 Are the sentences true or false?

	True	False
1 An audience is all the actors in a play.	☐	☐
2 A holiday resort is a shop where you go to book a holiday.	☐	☐
3 The lines in a play are the words the actors speak.	☐	☐
4 Your accommodation is the plane, boat, etc. that takes you to your holiday.	☐	☐
5 Actors have rehearsals to practise their performance.	☐	☐

Ways of communicating

describe	post	shout	translate	whisper
greet	shake hands	smile	wave	

2 Circle the correct words.

1 At the beginning of the trip, we were *posted* / *greeted* / *waved* by our tour guide.
2 I think he enjoyed the show because he was *shouting* / *waving* / *smiling*.
3 Alfonso will *describe* / *translate* / *whisper* all the tourist attractions we are going to see.
4 She plays the part of an angry teacher who *shouts* / *posts* / *smiles* at her students a lot.
5 In the first scene, two actors meet and *translate* / *shake hands* / *describe*.

LEARN TO LEARN

Personalising vocabulary

Writing personalised sentences helps you to learn new words.

3 Choose four verbs from the list above and write sentences that are true for you. Then tell your partner.

1 ______________________
2 ______________________
3 ______________________
4 ______________________

Our teacher greets us every morning.

1 VOCABULARY BANK

Describing clothes and shoes

baggy

checked

cotton

denim

flat

flowery

high-heeled

long-sleeved

plain

spotted

striped

tight

1 Is the adjective order correct or incorrect? Circle the correct answer.

1. We have to wear leather flat shoes. *Correct / Incorrect*
2. Paul was wearing a red baggy T-shirt. *Correct / Incorrect*
3. Laura bought a flowery cotton blouse. *Correct / Incorrect*
4. I'd like a denim black jacket. *Correct / Incorrect*
5. The singer wore tight striped trousers. *Correct / Incorrect*

Verbs related to clothes and shoes

do up fit fold	go out of fashion go with	hang up match suit	undo wear out

2 Circle the correct words.

1. I can't wear this spotted scarf. It doesn't *hang up / go with / fold* my coat.
2. This dress is a bit tight. It doesn't *match / undo / fit* me any more.
3. I've had this sweater for years. It never seems to *wear out / suit me / undo me.*
4. Don't leave your jacket on the floor. *Hang it up / Do it up / Wear it out* in your wardrobe.
5. You look great in that checked shirt. It really *goes out of fashion / suits you / goes with you.*

LEARN TO LEARN

Categorising

Recording new words in categories helps you to remember their meaning.

3 Put the clothes verbs above in the correct categories. Compare with a partner.

Putting clothes away	hang up
Ways of saying that clothes look good	
Reasons not to wear clothes	
Putting on and taking off clothes	

2 VOCABULARY BANK

Phrasal verbs: changes

do without	go back	look forward to	move to	sign up	turn down
end up	go through	move out	settle down	try out	turn out

1 Complete the statements with a phrasal verb from the list. Put them in order from most true for you (1) to least true for you (5). Compare with a partner.

1 I would love to ________ New York. ________
2 I never ________ party invitations. ________
3 I always ________ my English classes. ________
4 I like to ________ new video games with my friends. ________
5 I would like to ________ in one place for my whole life. ________

Parts of objects

button

cable

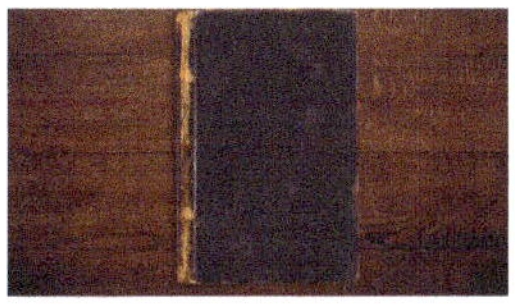
cover

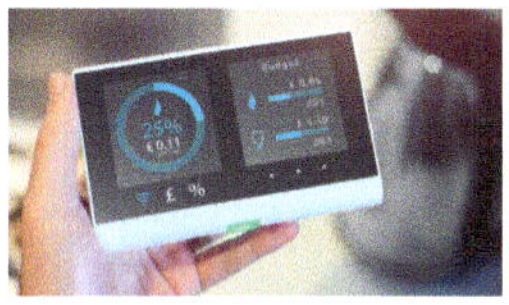
display

handle

key

lens

lid

plug

strap

2 Use the clues to find the mystery word. Write your own clue for the mystery word.

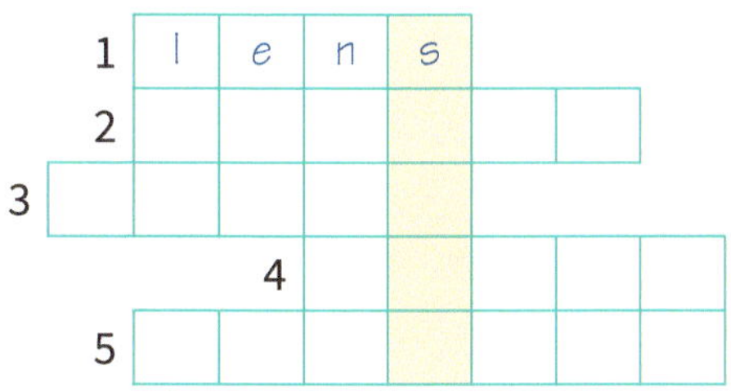

1 I'm made of glass. You look through me.
2 I am round. You press me to make a lift come.
3 I'm made of paper. I go on books to protect them.
4 I am long and thin. I bring electricity to objects.
5 I show information, for example the time.

Mystery word: ________ Your clue: ________________

LEARN TO LEARN

Visualising words in different situations

Visualising words in different situations helps you to remember them.

3 Where would you find these parts (1–4)? Use the objects from the box. Some may have more than one part. Then choose two more parts from the list above and think of objects that have them.

keyboard TV jam jar laptop vacuum cleaner saucepan door shoe box

1 key ________ 2 handle ________ 3 lid ________ 4 plug ________

3 VOCABULARY BANK

Cooking verbs

bake

chop

fry

grate

grill

heat

overcook

peel

roast

season

slice

spread

1 Put the verbs in the correct place so that this potato recipe makes sense.

First, [1]*season* the oven to 220°. [2]*Overcook* the potatoes and [3]*peel* them into large pieces. Add two spoonfuls of oil and [4]*heat* with some salt and pepper. [5]*Chop* the potatoes for 45 minutes, but be careful not to [6]*roast* them!

1 heat 2 ______ 3 ______ 4 ______ 5 ______ 6 ______

Quantities

a chunk of	a handful of	a piece of	a slice of	a spoonful of
a cup of	a packet of	a pinch of	a splash of	a sprinkle of

2 Match 1–5 with a–e.

1 This sauce isn't sweet enough. I'm going to add a spoonful of ______
2 I'm cooking tonight. We're having a lovely piece of ______
3 Grill the fish with a pinch of ______
4 I'm going to fry the potatoes with a splash of ______
5 The soup will be delicious because she's putting in a handful of ______

a sugar.
b oil.
c fresh herbs.
d beef.
e salt.

LEARN TO LEARN

Word partners

When you learn new words, try to learn words that go with them so that you can use them in natural contexts.

3 Choose four quantities and think of three food items to go with each one. Compare with a partner.

1 ______
2 ______
3 ______
4 ______

a chunk of cheese, meat, potato.

4 VOCABULARY BANK

The five senses

feel feel like	look look like	smell smell like	sound sound like	taste taste like	touch

1 **Complete the sentences with the words in the box.**

delicious stone a train fresh bread icy

1 Has someone been baking? It smells like ____________ in here.
2 It's actually wood, but it's so cold, it feels like ____________ .
3 I don't know what's in this dish, but it tastes ____________ .
4 I heard a loud noise. It sounded a bit like ____________ .
5 Be careful when you go outside. The pavement looks ____________ .

Describing texture, sound, taste, etc.

colourful

faint

rough

sharp

shiny

smelly

smooth

sour

spicy

transparent

2 **Match 1–5 with a–e.**

1 You've worn that shirt for three days. ________
2 Be careful with that knife. ________
3 The noise can't be coming from this room. ________
4 Antonio washed his car yesterday. ________
5 I think it must be lemon juice. ________

a It tastes rather sour.
b It's too faint.
c It must be a bit smelly.
d It looks very sharp.
e That's why it's so shiny.

LEARN TO LEARN

Brainstorming

Brainstorming word groups can help you make vocabulary connections.

3 **Choose three of the words from the list above and brainstorm connected words with your partner.**

1 ______________________________
2 ______________________________
3 ______________________________

shiny: shoes, hair, gold, metal, glass, car, clean.

5 VOCABULARY BANK

Processes

attract	communicate	create	develop	produce	supply
collect	connect	deliver	measure	solve	waste

1 Match 1–5 with a–e.

1 The parcel was delivered ________
2 This course will help you to develop ________
3 The new factory will create ________
4 I need to collect ________
5 We hope the museum will attract ________

a hundreds of jobs.
b to the wrong house.
c more tourists to the area.
d some books from the library.
e your communication skills.

Extreme adjectives

boiling

deafening

dreadful

enormous

fascinating

freezing

gorgeous

marvellous

stunning

terrifying

2 Put the letters in order to make extreme adjectives.

1 Before the electricity was connected, our house was *engefzir* in winter. ________
2 The crowd produced a *engafedni* noise. ________
3 They measured the bones and discovered that the creature was *eomosurn*. ________
4 It's *dafreuld* to waste so much water. ________
5 She's able to communicate difficult ideas in a *nafsatingci* way. ________

LEARN TO LEARN

Personalising new vocabulary

Using personalised sentences helps you to remember new vocabulary.

3 Choose four words from the list above and use them to write questions to ask your partner.

1 ____________________
2 ____________________
3 ____________________
4 ____________________

What is the most fascinating book you've ever read? *Treasure Island*

6 VOCABULARY BANK

Verb collocations with *get*, *take* and *have*

get a lot out of	get on my nerves	have fun	take an interest in
get bored	get to know	have the chance	take pleasure in
get lost	have doubts	take advantage of	take risks

1 Put the words in the correct order to make sentences.

1 better / know / to / I'd / her / get / like / to / . I think she's very interesting.

____

2 lot / Simon / course / got / a / of / the / out / . He said it was very useful.

____

3 the / at / picnic / you / did / fun / have / ? You certainly had good weather for it.

____

4 get / some / nerves / of / on / my / my / classmates / . They're quite annoying.

____

Inspiration and challenge

bravery (n)

challenge (n)

determination (n)

obstacle (n)

opportunity (n)

achieve (v)

encourage (v)

inspire (v)

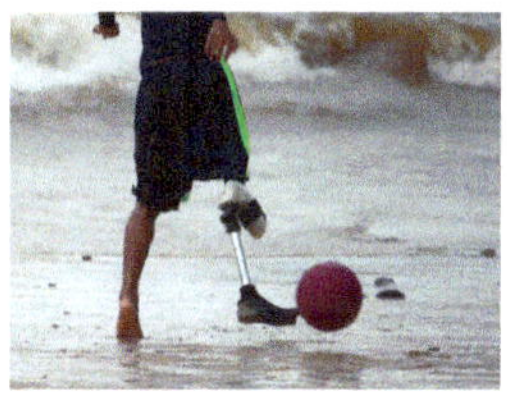
overcome (v)

support (v)

2 Underline the incorrect words in each sentence.

1 Harry managed to overcome the *problem* / *solution* / *obstacle*.
2 Mrs Betts always tries to encourage her *students* / *children* / *happiness*.
3 Luke has the determination to achieve his *salary* / *goals* / *ambition*.
4 I think we were all inspired by her *speech* / *bravery* / *disappointment*.

LEARN TO LEARN

Stress patterns

Knowing the stress pattern of a word can help you pronounce it and hear it when people say it.

3 Write the stress pattern for each word. The first one has been done for you.

1 bravery Ooo　　2 encourage ________　　3 opportunity ________

7 VOCABULARY BANK

Feelings

amused

annoyed

down

eager

glad

grateful

hopeful

hurt

insecure

peaceful

ridiculous

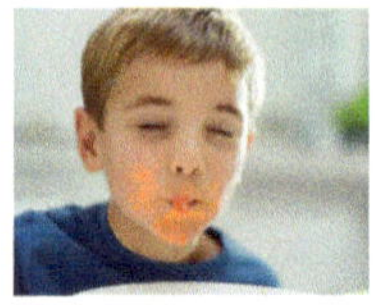
satisfied

thrilled

1 Complete the statements with the words in the box. Do you agree or disagree?

eager grateful insecure peaceful ridiculous

	Agree	Not sure	Disagree
1 I feel ________ when friends remember my birthday.	☐	☐	☐
2 I feel a bit ________ about the future.	☐	☐	☐
3 I feel ________ in a hat.	☐	☐	☐
4 I am always ________ to try new experiences.	☐	☐	☐
5 I feel ________ when I am in the countryside.	☐	☐	☐

Expressions with *heart* and *mind*

be in two minds bear in mind break someone's heart	change your mind close to your heart cross your mind	have something on your mind learn by heart	make your mind up put your heart into something

2 Circle the correct words.

1. Leaving my girlfriend behind in Australia *was close to my heart / broke my heart / changed my mind.*
2. I'm annoyed because you won't *make your mind up / learn by heart / cross your mind* about the party.
3. Winning was important to Max and he really *had it on his mind / bore it in mind / put his heart into it.*
4. I'm *in two minds / crossing my mind / bearing in mind* about telling my sister the truth.

LEARN TO LEARN

Gapped flashcards

Using gapped flashcards can help you learn expressions.

3 Use the flashcards you made in class. Take turns to pick up a flashcard, look at the front and make a sentence. Score two points for a correct sentence but lose a point if you look at the back.

I was going to go swimming but I ***changed my mind****.*

8 VOCABULARY BANK

Advertising

ad blocker
advert
advertise
brand
buyer
influence
logo
marketing company
product
review
seller
slogan

1 Complete the sentences with a noun from the same word family as the verb.

1. They're looking for someone to buy their company. They want a ________ .
2. Dan reviews hotels online. He writes ________ .
3. They advertise on the London Underground. They have ________ there.
4. She has a factory that produces mugs. Its ________ is mugs.
5. I'm not influenced by celebrity vloggers. They don't have any ________ on me.

Internet verbs

build up
comment on
delete
follow
post
shut down
subscribe
switch off
switch on
vlog

2 Use verbs from the list above to complete the questions. Ask and answer them.

1. Do you ________ anyone online?
2. What would influence you to ________ to an online magazine?
3. What subject does your favourite YouTuber ________ about?
4. Would you ________ an online comment if it upset a friend?
5. Do you ever ________ other people's posts?

LEARN TO LEARN

Collocations

When you learn a new verb, try to learn the nouns that go with it. This will help your English sound natural.

3 Match the verb 1–5 with its noun collocation a–e. Can you think of any other nouns that go with these verbs?

1 shut down — a followers
2 follow — b a post
3 build up — c a phone
4 switch off — d a vlogger
5 comment on — e an account

9 VOCABULARY BANK

Reporting verbs

admit	apologise	complain	deny	insist	refuse
announce	claim	confirm	discover	promise	suggest

1 Complete the sentences with the correct form of a reporting verb from the list above.

1 'I stole the money.' She ________ that she had stolen the money.
2 'The hotel was really dirty.' My mother ________ about the hotel.
3 'I'll definitely be back by nine o'clock.' Samantha ________ that she would be back by nine o'clock.
4 'I'm certainly not going to help.' Adam ________ to help us.
5 'I'm so sorry that I lied to you.' Tom ________ for lying.

Adverbs of time and manner

after a while	fluently	nowadays	patiently	secretly
eventually	gradually	occasionally	regularly	surprisingly

2 Circle the correct words.

1 They waited *secretly* / *patiently* / *gradually* for Max to arrive.
2 It was raining for hours but *eventually* / *regularly* / *nowadays* it stopped.
3 The food in the restaurant was *fluently* / *secretly* / *surprisingly* nice.
4 At first I found the lessons difficult, but *occasionally* / *after a while* / *regularly* I got better at them.
5 I went running every day and *fluently* / *patiently* / *gradually* I got fitter.

LEARN TO LEARN

Recording words in sentences

Writing down new words in a sentence helps you to remember them.

3 Choose four words from the list above and write sentences that are true for you. Then tell your partner.

1 ____________________
2 ____________________
3 ____________________
4 ____________________

I usually drink coffee but occasionally I drink tea.

2 HISTORY

1 Look at the title and picture and discuss the questions.
1 When do you think this picture was taken?
2 Where are the people and what are they doing?

2.14 2 Read the text. Check your answer to question 2 in Exercise 1.

STARTING AGAIN

Between 1880 and 1910, 17 million Europeans made the decision to move to the United States and start a new life. Many of them never went back to their country of birth. This was part of what is known as the Great Atlantic **Migration**. It started in the 1840s and it is the largest migration in history.

For many people, it was the first time they had ever left their hometown. The two-week journey was very unpleasant, and on larger ships up to 2,000 people were **crammed** into the lower **decks**. It was dark, there was little fresh water, and the air was **rancid**. So why choose to go through such a difficult experience?

One major reason was hunger. For example, in Ireland in the 1840s, people used to depend on potatoes for food. When the potato crop failed for three years in a row, there was not enough to eat and around one million people died. After this, half of the Irish population decided to move to the United States. They were nervous about the journey, but they looked forward to a better life.

> I am exceedingly well pleased at coming to this land of plenty.

Letter from an Irish immigrant to The Times, *London, 1850*

Immigrants from all over Europe had their own story to tell. Although they had never experienced life in the United States before, they arrived ready to **settle** in a new culture. Immigrants helped build the United States into the country it is today. Like all migrations, the Great Atlantic Migration is the story of people making difficult decisions for the chance to start again.

3 Read the text again. Write *T* (true), *F* (false) or *DS* (doesn't say).
1 Most immigrants to the United States eventually returned to their country of birth. ___
2 There wasn't much room on board the ships. ___
3 Poverty was a major reason for migration. ___
4 Irish immigrants felt hopeful about their future. ___
5 Immigrants from all over Europe moved for the same reasons as the Irish. ___
6 They made a positive contribution to American society. ___

4 Discuss other possible causes of migration throughout history and up to the present day.

5 Complete the definitions with the words in **bold** in the text.
1 ________ (n) the act of moving from one place to another
2 ________ (n) the floors of a ship
3 ________ (v) to make a home
4 ________ (v) to be filled with something so there is no more room
5 ________ (adj) having a very bad smell (or taste)

Explore it!

Guess the correct answer.

How many people live in a country different to the one they were born in?

a over 50 million
b over 150 million
c over 250 million

Find another interesting fact about migration. Write a question for your partner to answer.

4 SCIENCE

Echolocation

Imagine you are walking with a torch through a forest at night. Suddenly, the light goes out and you cannot see a thing. You feel a branch brush your face and smell the leaves on the trees. You need to go home, but how can you find your way?

If you were a bat, you would use echolocation. Echolocation is a technique used by some animals to move around in the dark. It helps them identify friends and enemies and 'see' where they are going. Here are two examples of how animals use it.

Dolphins

To identify objects in deep, dark waters, dolphins produce high-frequency **clicks**. These create sound waves that **bounce back** as echoes. This information helps dolphins work out the distance, direction of travel, speed and size of things.

Bats

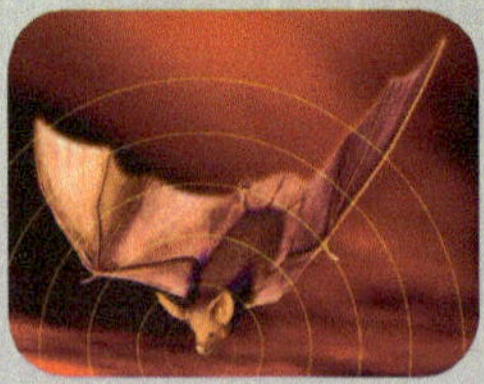

To hunt for insects in the dark, bats make a **high-pitched** call as they fly, then listen for the returning **echo**. They calculate how far away something is by how long it takes the echo to return. A bat can **detect** an insect in the dark from a distance of five metres!

But you don't have to be a bat or a dolphin to echolocate. You might be surprised to learn that some humans can echolocate too. One such person is Daniel Kish. Daniel is completely blind, so he gets information about what is around him by clicking his tongue and listening to the echo. This technique allows him to safely ride a bike or go hiking in the wild. He also trains other blind people to echolocate. Amazing, isn't it?

1 Discuss the questions.

1 What special skills do the animals in the pictures have?

2 What do they use these skills for?

4.10 **2 Read the article. Check your answers to Exercise 1.**

3 Complete the table with information from the article.

	Sound	How it helps
Bat	1	4
Dolphin	2	5
Daniel Kish	3	6

4 Complete the text with the words in bold in the article.

Whales, like dolphins, produce [1]________ to work out an object's distance, direction, speed and size. These sounds can be low- or [2]________. The sounds hit an object and [3]________ to the whale's throat. The time it takes the [4]________ of these sounds to return to the whale helps the animal to [5]________, or sense, what is around it.

Explore it!

Guess the correct answer.

Some bats have a scream as loud as a …

a jet engine 30 metres away.

b very loud opera singer.

c machine that breaks rocks.

Find another interesting fact about bats, whales or echolocation. Write a question for your partner to answer.

6 CITIZENSHIP

1 **Discuss the questions.**

1. What is digital citizenship?
2. How can the way we use technology affect our relationships with people?

2 6.12 **Read the article. Check your answers to Exercise 1.**

3 **Read the nine themes of digital citizenship and mark (✓) the ones that apply to each case study. Some apply to both and some to neither.**

Nine Themes of Digital Citizenship	CS1	CS2
1 Have equal access to technology.	✗	✗
2 Buy and sell safely online.		
3 Share information safely.		
4 Learn how to use technology appropriately.		
5 Follow an ethical code of conduct.		
6 Use technology lawfully.		
7 Act responsibly.		
8 Promote physical and psychological well-being.		
9 Protect online safety.		

4 **Discuss the questions in the case studies in the article.**

5 **Complete the sentences with the words in bold in the article.**

1. That is a very ________ photo. You look great!
2. You cannot ________ some websites to be safe. You should check your online privacy.
3. Please don't ________ me. Turn off your phone and listen to what I am saying.
4. I am going to ________ how often I use social media. I want to use it less.
5. He is always very polite and ________ when he sends messages.

Digital citizenship: case studies

Today's citizens can make the most of living, learning, and working in a digital world. However, this brings responsibilities as well as opportunities, as these digital citizens need to act in a safe, legal, and ethical way. Digital citizenship is similar to traditional citizenship in that it means being kind, **respectful** and ready to take part in activities that make the world a better place.

If teens take risks with the way they use digital devices, it could lead to problems. These case studies illustrate some common situations.

Case study 1

Some friends are having fun at the beach. Later, one of them posts photos of the others online. She does not ask permission and some of the pictures are not very **flattering**. If you had been in possession of these pictures, what would you have done?

Case study 2

A group of friends are sitting in a café. One of them gets a call on his phone. He answers the call, **ignores** his friends, and has a loud, personal conversation in front of them. How would you feel if you were in the group?

The way these people use technology raises serious questions about **trust**, friendship and social relationships.

Digital citizenship involves many things, from sharing information safely to acting responsibly online. If we want to get the best out of a fast-changing world, we should **monitor** our digital habits. In this way we can meet the challenge of becoming good digital citizens.

Explore it!

Guess the correct answer.

In an average lifetime, people will spend … on social media.

a one year and two months
b three years and five months
c five years and four months

Find another interesting fact about the digital world. Write a question for your partner to answer.

8 ART AND DESIGN

1 Discuss the questions.

1 Where do you see print adverts?
2 How do print adverts communicate their messages?
3 What are the main elements of a print advert?

8.11 **2 Read the article. Check your answers to Exercise 1.**

How to design an effective print advert

We are surrounded by print adverts. When we walk down the street, there are slogans, logos and images everywhere. Think about how many adverts you have seen today. How many of them can you actually remember?

Marketing companies, which are responsible for advertising campaigns, charge a lot of money for their services. Therefore, a printed message needs to effectively communicate a brand's image. In fact, the person who creates an advert is a communicator more than a designer. So how is an **effective** print advert designed?

The **headline** is the most important element. An advert has approximately two seconds to catch the reader's eye, so the headline needs to be clear and focus on one idea. A **subhead**, which still needs to be brief, can then give more information.

Next is the image. Sometimes an image can become the centre of attention and distract from the message of a print advert. The headline and image need to work well together and it is essential that the image is relevant to the product. Also, advertising research shows men and women respond to images differently. Many advertisers use brighter colours in adverts for women and darker shapes in adverts for men.

Once an advert has these features, it is time to decide on a final **layout**. The top-to-bottom layout in the picture, which is widely used, is very effective. Most adverts influence potential buyers with the most important information at the top.

A good advert tells us we need things that previously we didn't even know existed. Next time you walk down a street full of print adverts, think about how effective they are.

3 Complete the sentences with your own ideas.

1 Marketing companies need to effectively communicate a brand's image because …
2 A headline is the most important element of a print advert because …
3 An image should not be the main focus of a print advert because …
4 Different images are used for men and women in print adverts because …

4 Choose an idea and turn it into a headline of three or four words for an advert.

1 This toothpaste will leave your mouth fresh and clean and your teeth white.
2 You must buy these jeans because they are more comfortable and cheaper than others.

____

____

5 Complete the definitions with the words in bold in the article.

1 ________ (n) the design of something
2 ________ (n) the title written in big letters
3 ________ (n) heading that comes after the headline
4 ________ (adj) successful

Explore it!

Guess the correct answer.

More than … a year is spent on advertising.

a $6 billion b $60 billion c $600 billion

Find another interesting fact about advertising. Write a question for your partner to answer.

PRONUNCIATION

UNIT 1

The letters *ea*

1.08 **1 Listen and repeat.**

1 /eə/ wear 2 /e/ bread 3 /iː/ meat 4 /eɪ/ steak

2 Put the words in the correct column according to the pronunciation of the letters *ea*.

break clean great head heaven peach ~~pear~~ please weather

/eə/	/e/	/iː/	/eɪ/
pear			

1.09 **3 Listen, check and repeat.**

UNIT 2

used to

2.04 **1 Listen and repeat.**

1 He used to go out with his friends every weekend.
2 Did you use to like cats when you were younger?

2.05 **2 Listen to the sentences. Are the words in bold pronounced the same in each sentence?**

1 She **used a** friend's phone to call her parents.
2 She **used to** have her mum's phone.

2.06 **3 Listen and write the sentences.**

1 ______
2 ______
3 ______
4 ______

4 Practise saying the sentences.

1 She used to play football after school.
2 My dad used to listen to classical music.
3 Did you use to live here?

2.07 **5 Listen and check.**

UNIT 3

The letters *ch*

3.03 **1 Listen and repeat.**

1 /ʃ/ machine 2 /tʃ/ cheese 3 /k/ school

2 Put the words in the correct column according to the pronunciation of the letters *ch*

check **ch**emistry **ch**orus head**ach**e me**ch**anic ~~moustache~~ para**ch**ute rea**ch** sear**ch** tou**ch**

/ʃ/	/tʃ/	/k/
moustache		

3.04 **3 Listen, check and repeat.**

UNIT 4

Weak form of *to*

4.06 **1 Listen and repeat.**

1 He has to work late tonight.
2 I need to buy new shoes.
3 We ought to take an umbrella.

4.07 **2 Listen and underline the stressed words.**

1 I'd like to know what time the film starts.
2 We have to leave early tomorrow.
3 You ought to study more for your exams.
4 Do you need to make a phone call?

4.07 **3 Listen, check and repeat.**

4 Practise saying the sentences with the correct pronunciation of *to*.

1 Do you think we ought to tell him?
2 Erin needs to go food shopping.
3 I'd like to go to the party but my mum says I have to stay home.

UNIT 5

The letters *mb* and *bt*

5.07 **1 Listen and repeat.**

1 She's a climber. 2 I doubt he's coming.

2 Circle the silent *b* in each sentence.

1 I saw a film about a bomb.
2 I haven't got any debts.
3 He hurt his thumb with a hammer.
4 I saw a sheep with two lambs.

5.08 **3 Listen, check and repeat.**

UNIT 6

Stress in multi-syllable words

6.02 **1 Listen and repeat.**

1 temperature 2 different 3 comfortable

6.03 **2 Underline the stressed syllable in each word. Listen and check.**

1 interesting 4 category 7 vegetable
2 Wednesday 5 chocolate 8 memorable
3 business 6 secondary

3 Identify the syllables which are not pronounced.

1 interesting

4 Practise saying the words in Exercise 2.

UNIT 7

Initial consonant clusters with *s*

7.07 **1 Listen and repeat.**

1 stress 3 strength
2 strong 4 straight

7.08 **2 Listen and repeat the tongue-twisters.**

1 **Strong** winds **spread** the sparks through the **streets**.
2 Stella's got **straight** hair and **stripes** on her skirt.
3 Stuart **sprayed** his phone with a **screen** cleaner.

7.09 **3 Listen, repeat and practise the words.**

UNIT 8

The letters *-tion*

8.04 **1 Listen and repeat.**

1 /ʃən/ celebration 2 /tʃən/ suggestion

2 Look at the *-tion* ending in the words. Write *1* (/ʃən/) or *2* (/tʃən/).

1 position 1 5 connection ___
2 digestion ___ 6 question ___
3 contribution ___ 7 indigestion ___
4 vacation ___

8.05 **3 Listen, check and repeat.**

4 Answer the questions.

1 What's your idea of the perfect celebration?
2 What question would you like to ask your favourite celebrity?
3 Where would you go for your ideal vacation?

UNIT 9

The letters *cia*

9.02 **1 Listen and repeat.**

1 social 3 musician 5 commercial
2 sociable 4 special

2 Practise saying the words.

1 magician 4 politician
2 beneficial 5 mathematician
3 artificial

9.03 **3 Listen, check and repeat.**

4 Student A reads a definition. Student B says the correct word from Exercises 1 or 2.

1 When someone likes meeting new people.
2 Someone who likes numbers.
3 Something good and useful.
4 Someone who plays an instrument.
5 Not real or natural.
6 Someone who takes a rabbit out of a hat.

IRREGULAR VERBS

Infinitive	Past simple	Past participle
be	was/were	been
beat	beat	beaten
become	became	become
begin	began	begun
bite	bit	bitten
blow	blew	blown
break	broke	broken
bring	brought	brought
build	built	built
buy	bought	bought
catch	caught	caught
choose	chose	chosen
come	came	come
cost	cost	cost
cut	cut	cut
do	did	done
draw	drew	drawn
drink	drank	drunk
drive	drove	driven
eat	ate	eaten
fall	fell	fallen
feel	felt	felt
fight	fought	fought
find	found	found
fly	flew	flown
forget	forgot	forgotten
get	got	got
give	gave	given
go	went	gone
grow	grew	grown
hang	hung	hung
have	had	had
hear	heard	heard
hide	hid	hidden
hit	hit	hit
hold	held	held
hurt	hurt	hurt
keep	kept	kept
know	knew	known
leave	left	left
lend	lent	lent

Infinitive	Past simple	Past participle
let	let	let
lie	lied	lied
light	lit	lit
lose	lost	lost
make	made	made
mean	meant	meant
meet	met	met
pay	paid	paid
put	put	put
read	read	read
ride	rode	ridden
ring	rang	rung
rise	rose	risen
run	ran	run
say	said	said
see	saw	seen
sell	sold	sold
send	sent	sent
shine	shone	shone
shoot	shot	shot
show	showed	shown
shut	shut	shut
sing	sang	sung
sit	sat	sat
sleep	slept	slept
speak	spoke	spoken
spend	spent	spent
stand	stood	stood
steal	stole	stolen
swim	swam	swum
take	took	taken
teach	taught	taught
tear	tore	torn
tell	told	told
think	thought	thought
throw	threw	thrown
understand	understood	understood
wake	woke	woken
wear	wore	worn
win	won	won
write	wrote	written

Acknowledgements

The authors and publishers acknowledge the following sources of copyright material and are grateful for the permissions granted. While every effort has been made, it has not always been possible to identify the sources of all the material used, or to trace all copyright holders. If any omissions are brought to our notice, we will be happy to include the appropriate acknowledgements on reprinting & in the next update to the digital edition, as applicable.

Key: CLIL = Content and Language Integrated Learning; SU = Starter Unit; U = Unit, VB = Vocabulary Bank.

Text

U1: Text about Moziah Bridge. Copyrighyt © Adriann Ranta Zurhellen. Reproduced with permission; **U04:** Text about Neil Harbisson. Copyright © Neil Harbisson. Reproduced with kind permission; Text about surfer Bethany Hamilton. Copyright © Becky Hamilton. Reproduced with kind permission.

Photography

The following photographs are sourced from Getty Images.

SU: Dave and Les Jacobs/Blend Images; Django/E+; jhorrocks/E+; Vostok/Moment; Lennart Schreiber/EyeEm; Adie Bush/Cultura; Hill Street Studios/Blend Images; vetdoctor/iStock/Getty Images Plus; yayayoyo/iStock/Getty Images Plus; Tigatelu/iStock/Getty Images Plus Elizabeth Parsons/EyeEm Premium John Lawson, Belhaven/Moment Open Yavuz Meyveci/iStock Editorial/Getty Images Plus; arabianEye arabianEye; **U1:** DigiPub/Moment Open; Henrik Sorensen/Stone; Halfpoint/iStock/Getty Images Plus; Halfpoint/iStock/Getty Images Plus; Timur Emek/Getty Images Entertainment; Maciej Frolow/The Image Bank; Artur Debat/Moment Mobile; Sidekick/E+; Pascal Deloche/Godong/Corbis Documentary; Chris Ryan/OJO Images; Andy Crawford/Dorling Kindersley; khvost/iStock/Getty Images Plus; GeorgePeters/E+; Paul Simcock; Erik Isakson; Feifei Cui-Paoluzzo/Moment; Hans-Peter Merten/The Image Bank; jboater/iStock/Getty Images Plus; PeterHermesFurian/iStock/Getty Images Plus; Rohappy/iStock/Getty Images Plus; Leon Bennett/WireImage; ozgurdonmaz/iStock/Getty Images Plus; mocoo/iStock/Getty Images Plus; **U2:** Jennifer Perry/EyeEm; mantaphoto/E+; Mark Daffey/Lonely Planet Images; KIKILOMBO/iStock/Getty Images Plus; alejandrophotography/iStock/Getty Images Plus; Emanuele Ravecca/EyeEm; Science Photo Library; luoman/E+; Spod/iStock/Getty Images Plus; Steve Shott/Dorling Kindersley; Gregory_DUBUS/iStock/Getty Images Plus; DNY59/E+; Oleg Golovnev/EyeEm; Westend61; Betsie Van der Meer/Stone; ajr_images/iStock/Getty Images Plus; pixdeluxe/iStock/Getty Images Plus; LisaAFischer/iStock/Getty Images Plus; H. Armstrong Roberts/ClassicStock/Archive Photos; H. Armstrong Roberts/ClassicStock/Archive Photos; Allan Tannenbaum/Archive Photos; Michael Ochs Archives; funky-data/E+; cjmacer/iStock Editorial/Getty Images Plus; mocoo/iStock/Getty Images Plus; **U3:** WIN-Initiative; tgasser/iStock/Getty Images Plus; BravissimoS/iStock/Getty Images Plus; EasterBunnyUK/iStock/Getty Images Plus; Valentyn Semenov/EyeEm; DonNichols/iStock/Getty Images Plus; mikroman6/Moment; Eskay Lim/EyeEm; Jamie Grill/The Image Bank; Bill Oxford/E+; Capelle.r/Moment; Jamie Stamey/iStock/Getty Images Plus; Ian Cuming/Ikon Images; NosUA/iStock/Getty Images Plus; D-Keine/E+; Andrey Suslov/iStock/Getty Images Plus; Sirikunkrittaphuk/iStock/Getty Images Plus; Creativ Studio Heinemann; Slawomir Tomas/EyeEm; Maximilian Stock Ltd./Photographer's Choice; Hayley Harrison/The Image Bank; Dorling Kindersley; GorynVD/iStock/Getty Images Plus; William Whitehurst/Corbis; Blend Images - KidStock/Brand X Pictures; KidStock/Blend Images; Maica/iStock/Getty Images Plus; Diana Miller/Cultura; Peter Cade/The Image Bank; marilyna/iStock/Getty Images Plus; Tetra Images; Tobias Titz; Hauke Dressler/LOOK-foto/LOOK; Neydtstock/iStock/Getty Images Plus; Melanitta/iStock/Getty Images Plus; Jami Tarris/Corbis Documentary; GMVozd/E+; Image Source; Tanya Zouev/StockFood Creative; Neustockimages/iStock/Getty Images Plus; Tim Platt/The Image Bank; Westend61; Rasulovs/iStock/Getty Images Plus; WoodyUpstate/iStock/Getty Images Plus; vovashevchuk/iStock/Getty Images Plus; Joff Lee/Photolibrary; Rosemary Calvert/Photographer's Choice; petekarici/E+; Jbryson/iStock/Getty Images Plus; mocoo/iStock/Getty Images Plus; **U4:** Buena Vista Images/DigitalVision; Alberto Ghizzi Panizza/Biosphoto; Arrow/DigitalVision; manoa/Moment; Paula Daniëlse/Moment Open; Tony Robins/Photolibrary; Andy Sotiriou/Photodisc; Tai/Moment; Raimund Linke/Oxford Scientific; bugphai/iStock/Getty Images Plus; Jamie Brand/EyeEm; Ian O'Leary/Dorling Kindersley; Sam Edwards/Sam Edwards; Danita Delimont/Gallo Images; Jutta Klee/Canopy; Jacqui Hurst/Photolibrary; hphimagelibrary/Gallo Images; Foodcollection; Christian Adams/Photographer's Choice; Coleman515/iStock/Getty Images Plus; DragonImages/iStock/Getty Images Plus; bergamont/iStock/Getty Images Plus; Stephen Stickler/Photographer's Choice; Kirshal/iStock/Getty Images Plus Douglas Sacha/Moment; Natthakan Jommanee/EyeEm; kiankhoon/iStock/Getty Images Plus; c11yg/iStock/Getty Images Plus; Copyright © Neil Harbisson. Reproduced with kind permission; Bruce Mclean/EyeEm; AVIcons/iStock/Getty Images Plus; Amin Yusifov/iStock/Getty Images Plus; mocoo/iStock/Getty Images Plus; **U5:** Satyan Chawla/500px Prime; Elena Pueyo/Moment; Andyworks/iStock/Getty Images Plus; Peter Schaefer/EyeEm; urfinguss/iStock/Getty Images Plus; Fabien_Gouby/iStock/Getty Images Plus; DiyanaDimitrova/iStock/Getty Images Plus; pskeltonphoto/Moment; chombosan/iStock/Getty Images Plus; Kitti Boonnitrod/Moment; HandmadePictures/iStock/Getty Images Plus; Ringo_Wong_hkherper/iStock/Getty Images Plus; Stígur Már Karlsson/Heimsmyndir/E+; DEA PICTURE LIBRARY/De Agostini; NASA/SCIENCE PHOTO LIBRARY; Creative Crop/Photodisc; Robin-Angelo Photography/Moment; Olivia ZZ/Moment; IndiaPictures/Universal Images Group; kajornyot/iStock/Getty Images Plus; kickimages/iStock/Getty Images Plus; Nitish Waila/iStock/Getty Images Plus; Amos Chapple/Lonely Planet Images; Anton Jankovoy/Moment; kdshutterman/iStock/Getty Images Plus; Shin Okamoto/Moment; Dorling Kindersley; mocoo/iStock/Getty Images Plus; **U6:** dennisvdw/iStock/Getty Images Plus; Philip Lee Harvey/The Image Bank; egon69/E+; Noel Hendrickson/DigitalVision; Andersen Ross Photography Inc/DigitalVision; Igor Emmerich/Cultura; Scott Sansenbach - Sansenbach Marine Photo/Moment; Lawrence Lucier/FilmMagic; Blend Images - Erik Isakson; dtiberio/iStock/Getty Images Plus; Juice Images Ltd; SolStock/E+; Frank Wijn/Moment Open; rozelt/iStock/Getty Images Plus; lvcandy/DigitalVision Vectors; mocoo/iStock/Getty Images Plus; **U7:** martin-dm/E+; bestdesigns/iStock/Getty Images Plus; BrianAJackson/iStock/Getty Images Plus; kgtoh/iStock/Getty Images Plus; Spohn Matthieu/PhotoAlto Agency RF Collections; Siphotography/iStock/Getty Images Plus; KatarzynaBialasiewicz/iStock/Getty Images Plus; Maskot; Ismailciydem/iStock/Getty Images Plus; mocoo/iStock/Getty Images Plus; **U8:** Juanmonino/iStock/Getty Images Plus; Hero Images; JohnnyGreig/E+; filo/DigitalVision Vectors; Diy13/iStock/Getty Images Plus; Milkos/iStock/Getty Images Plus; SPL IMAGES/Photographer's Choice; monkeybusinessimages/iStock/Getty Images Plus; photo/iStock/Getty Images Plus; robertiez/iStock/Getty Images Plus; Julian Kreler/EyeEm; mocoo/iStock/Getty Images Plus; **U9:** Hero Images; XiFotos/E+; sarah5/iStock/Getty Images Plus; photosindia; kelly bowden/Moment; chameleonseye/iStock/Getty Images Plus; Westend61; Hero Images; mocoo/iStock/Getty Images Plus; **VB:** Anthony Lee/OJO Images; vgajic/E+; Rafael Ben-Ari/The Image Bank; Imgorthand/E+; Asia-Pacific Images Studio/iStock/Getty Images Plus; Watchara Panyajun/EyeEm; majaiva/E+; Caiaimage/Sam Edwards; LeoPatrizi/E+; Brian Feinzimer/Getty Images Entertainment; domin_domin/iStock/Getty Images Plus; kitthanes/iStock/Getty Images Plus; Floortje/E+; olga_sweet/iStock/Getty Images Plus; Lalouetto/iStock/Getty Images Plus; Mehmet Hilmi Barcin/E+; FlamingPumpkin/iStock/Getty Images Plus; mawielobob/iStock/Getty Images Plus; Ng Sok Lian/EyeEm; Tarzhanova/iStock/Getty Images Plus; Karl Tapales/Moment; Melanie Hobson/EyeEm; kk2s/iStock/Getty Images Plus; MartinPrescott/E+; Gado Images/Photodisc; TARIK KIZILKAYA/E+; Jorge Alberto Bohorquez Suarez/EyeEm; LeMusique/iStock/Getty Images Plus; JohnGollop/E+; JuergenBosse/iStock/Getty Images Plus; tirc83/iStock/Getty Images Plus; KucherAV/iStock/Getty Images Plus; dlewis33/E+; Lucy Lambriex/DigitalVision; Adam Radosavljevic/EyeEm; Claire Gunn; lolostock/iStock/Getty Images Plus; uuurska/iStock/Getty Images Plus; Lakshmi3/iStock/Getty Images Plus; Westend61; Yurikr/iStock/Getty Images Plus; Paula ./FOAP; Dalia Rady/EyeEm; DragonFly/iStock/Getty Images Plus; Pierre-Yves Babelon/Antananarivo, Antananarivo Province, Madagascar; Mike Whitby/EyeEm; DAJ; Cody Duncan; Stefka Pavlova/Moment; Theerapan Bhumirat/EyeEm; luknaja/iStock/Getty Images Plus; Rachan Panya/EyeEm; erhui1979/DigitalVision Vectors; RapidEye/E+; Martin Diebel; Vicki Jauron, Babylon and Beyond Photography/Moment; sturti/E+; Marina Malikova/500px; ralucahphotography.ro/Moment; MaximShebeko/iStock/Getty Images Plus; Baac3nes/Moment; Johannes Hulsch/EyeEm Premium; Muhammad Faidz Zainal Abidin/EyeEm; deimagine/E+; BJI/Blue Jean Images; Sam Edwards/Caiaimage; PhotoAlto/Eric Audras/PhotoAlto Agency RF Collections; digitalskillet/iStock/Getty Images Plus; Chris Whitehead/Cultura; Caiaimage/Martin Barraud; Ricardo Lim/Moment Unreleased; Indeed; Plume Creative/DigitalVision; MediaProduction/E+; Elva Etienne/Moment; Mordolff/E+; Mint Images - Tim Robbins; Jose Luis Pelaez Inc/DigitalVision; xavierarnau/E+; Daisy-Daisy/iStock/Getty Images Plus; Emilija Manevska/Moment; slavemotion/E+; Paul Bradbury/OJO Images; Tom Merton/Caiaimage; moodboard/Cultura; littleny/iStock Editorial/Getty Images Plus; mikroman6/Moment; Maskot; **CLIL:** Bettmann; VICTOR HABBICK VISIONS/SCIENCE PHOTO LIBRARY; SeventyFour/iStock/Getty Images Plus; paseven/iStock/Getty Images Plus.

The following photographs are sourced from other libraries/sources.

U4: courtesy of Peter Cernik MA; **ICONS:** Prithvi/Noun Project; Agni/Noun Project; mikicon/Noun Project; Baboon designs, US/Noun Project; Tanguy Keryhuel, FR/Noun Project; Icons Bazaar/Noun Project; Adrien Coquet, FR/Noun Project; Vectors Market/Noun Project; TukTuk Design/Noun Project; iconsphere, ID/Noun Project; i cons, US/Noun Project; kim Eriksson/Noun Project; Lloyd Humphreys, DK/Noun Project; Delwar Hossain, BD/Noun Project; Kirby Wu, TW/Noun Project; Magicon, HU/Noun Project; Baboon designs, US/Noun Project.

Illustration

Caire Rollet (Illustration Web): **U2**, **U8**, **U9**, **EM**; Joanna Kerr: **U2**, **U4**; Sean Longcroft: **SU**, **U5**.